INTRODUCTION AND SUPPLEMENTAL INFORMATI

Target Audience

The Intermediate Fetal Monitoring Course is designed for perinatal clinicians who have completed a basic or foundations FHM course and who utilize fetal monitoring technology in the intrapartum setting. Clinicians whose only experience is antepartum in patient care, antepartum fetal heart assessment, or limited intrapartum care may need additional didactic and/or clinical experience to gain the required knowledge base. Physicians and Residents may attend this program and receive continuing medical education credit for full participation. It is expected that the participant already has basic knowledge and related skills in the following areas:

- Maternal physiologic changes of pregnancy
- Fetal growth and development
- Methods of fetal monitoring
- Preparation of patients for initiation of external or internal fetal monitoring
- Obtaining and maintaining tracings that document fetal heart rate and uterine contractions
- Interpretation of uterine contraction frequency, duration, intensity and baseline resting tone
- Identification of the baseline fetal heart rate, variability and variations
- Indicated clinical interventions
- Communication and documentation strategies

This course is based on educational theory and the instructional design incorporates critical thinking and decision making. To facilitate successful completion of the course, participants are expected, prior to attending the course, to review the current edition of *Fetal Heart Monitoring Principles and Practices* (print or e-book version). Although the content of this course is comprehensive, specific patient care responsibilities vary according to institution, state, province or region. Those individuals who participate in this course are advised to be familiar with their organizational/institutional responsibilities, as well as competence criteria and measurement.

Acknowledgment of Commercial Support

This CNE/CME activity has been created without commercial support.

Sponsorship and Co-Providership Statements

The CNE activity is provided by the Association of Women's Health, Obstetric and Neonatal Nurses (AWHONN) in collaboration with co-provider, Professional Education Services Group (PESG).

This activity has been planned and implemented in accordance with the Essential Areas and policies of the Accreditation Council for Continuing Medical Education through the joint sponsorship of the Professional Education Services Group (PESG) and the Association of Women's Health, Obstetric and Neonatal Nurses (AWHONN). The Professional Education Services Group is accredited by the ACCME to provide continuing medical education for physicians.

Learning Objectives

At the conclusion of this continuing education activity, participants will:
- Assess electronic fetal monitoring (EFM) tracings utilizing NICHD terminology.
- Interpret EFM tracings, analyze uterine activity and discuss the implications of contractions for fetal oxygenation.

- Describe clinical interventions and the related maternal-fetal physiology.
- Effectively communicate patient data through verbal and documentation methods.
- Describe roles and responsibilities of health care providers when using fetal monitoring in intrapartum care.

Content Validation Statement

It is the policy of AWHONN and PESG to review that the content contained in this CNE/CME activity is based on sound, scientific, evidence-based clinical practice. All recommendations involving clinical practice in this CNE/CME activity are based on evidence that is accepted within the professions of medicine and nursing as adequate justification for their indications and contraindications in the care of patients. AWHONN and PESG further assert that all scientific research referred to, reported or used in this CNE/CME activity in support or justification of a patient care recommendation conforms to the generally accepted standards of experimental design, data collection and analysis. Moreover, AWHONN and PESG establish that the content contained herein conforms to the definition of CNE as defined by the American Nurses Credentialing Center (ANCC) and the definition of CME as defined by the Accreditation Council for Continuing Medical Education (ACCME).

Disclosure Statement

It is the policy of Professional Education Services Group and the Association of Women's Health, Obstetric and Neonatal Nurses that the faculty and program planners and developers disclose real or apparent conflicts of interest relating to the topics of this education activity. Detailed disclosures must be made available during the live course.

Conflict of Interest Resolution Statement

When individuals in a position to control content have reported financial, professional or personal relationships with one or more commercial interests, AWHONN and PESG will resolve such conflicts to ensure that the presentation is free from commercial bias. The content of this presentation was vetted by the following mechanisms and modified as required to meet this standard:

- Content peer review by external topic expert
- Content validation by external topic expert and internal AWHONN and PESG clinical staff

Educational Peer Review Disclosure PESG and AWHONN report the following:

- **George J. Vuturo, RPh, PhD**
  CME Director
  Dr. Vuturo has no relevant financial relationships to disclose.
- **Frank Henry Boehm, MD**
  Dr. Boehm has no relevant financial relationships to disclose.
- **Susan Drummond, RN, MSN, C-EFM**
  Ms. Drummond has no relevant financial relationships to disclose.
- **Susan Bellebaum, RNC, MSN**
  Ms. Bellebaum has no relevant financial relationships to disclose.
- **Carol Elaine Brown, RN, BC, MNC-EFM**
  Nurse Program Development Specialist, AWHONN
  Ms. Brown has no relevant financial relationships to disclose.

SIXTH EDITION

INTERMEDIATE FETAL MONITORING COURSE

Student Materials

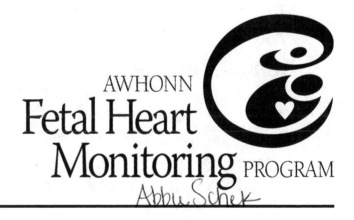

AWHONN
Fetal Heart
Monitoring PROGRAM

Abbie Schek

AWHONN
PROMOTING THE HEALTH OF
WOMEN AND NEWBORNS

Kendall Hunt
publishing company

C O N T E N T S

Accreditation Information

Association of Women's Health, Obstetric and Neonatal Nurses is accredited as a provider of continuing nursing education by the American Nurses Credentialing Center's Commission on Accreditation.

AWHONN also holds a California BRN number: California CNE provider #CEP580.

Accredited status does not imply endorsement by the provider or ANCC of any commercial products displayed or discussed in conjunction with an activity.

The maximum CNE credit that can be earned while attending the Intermediate Fetal Heart Monitoring Course is 18 AWHONN contact hours. Participants must attend the entire course and complete the feedback document in order to receive the CNE credit.

Accreditation Statement—Physicians

This activity has been planned and implemented in accordance with the accreditation requirements and policies of the Accreditation Council for Continuing Medical Education (ACCME) through the joint providership of Professional Education Services Group and the Association of Women's Health, Obstetric and Neonatal Nurses (AWHONN). Professional Education Services Group is accredited by the ACCME to provide continuing medical education for physicians.

Credit Designation Statement—Physicians

Professional Education Services Group designates this educational activity for a maximum of 15.25 *AMA PRA Category 1 Credits*™. Physicians should only claim credit within the extent of their participation in the activity.

DISCLAIMER

This course and all accompanying materials (publication) were developed by AWHONN in cooperation with PESG, as an educational resource for fetal heart monitoring. It presents general methods and techniques of practice that are currently acceptable, based on current research and used by recognized authorities. Proper care of individual patients may depend on many individual factors to be considered in clinical practice, as well as professional judgment in the techniques described herein. Clinical circumstances naturally vary, and professionals must use their own best judgment in accordance with the patients' needs and preferences, professional standards and institutional rules. Variations and innovations that are consistent with law, and that demonstrably improve the quality of patient care, should be encouraged.

AWHONN has sought to confirm the accuracy of the information presented herein and to describe generally accepted practices. However, AWHONN is not responsible for errors or omissions or for any consequences from application of the information in this resource and makes no warranty, expressed or implied, with respect to the contents of the publication. Competent clinical practice depends on a broad array of personal characteristics, training, judgment, professional skills and institutional processes. This publication is simply one of many information resources. This publication is not intended to replace ongoing evaluation of knowledge and skills in the clinical setting. Nor has it been designed for use in hiring, promotion or termination decisions or in resolving legal disputes or issues of liability.

AWHONN believes that drug selection and dosage set forth in this text are in accordance with current recommendations and practice at the time of publication.

However, in view of ongoing research, changes in government regulations and the constant flow of information relating to drug therapy and drug reactions, the reader is urged to check other information available in other published sources for each drug for potential changes in indications, dosages and for added warnings and precautions. This is particularly important when the recommended agent is a new or infrequently employed drug. In addition, appropriate medication use may depend on unique factors such as individuals' health status, other medication use and other factors which the professional must consider in clinical practice.

RESOURCES AND REFERENCE MATERIALS

The information within this section is provided to assist in your preparation for participation in the AWHONN Intermediate Fetal Monitoring Course.

The references were utilized in preparing the course content and may serve as additional resources for you during your course participation and in your clinical practice.

FETAL HEART RATE CHARACTERISTICS AND PATTERNS: 2008 NICHD DESCRIPTIVE TERMS FOR FETAL HEART RATE CHARACTERISTICS

Term	Definition
Baseline Rate	Approximate mean FHR rounded to increments of 5 bpm during a 10-minute segment, excluding accelerations and decelerations and periods of marked variability. In any 10-minute window, the minimum baseline duration must be at least 2 minutes (not necessarily contiguous) or the baseline for that period is indeterminate. In this case, one may need to refer to the previous 10-minute segment for determination of the baseline.
Bradycardia	Baseline rate of <110 bpm.
Tachycardia	Baseline rate of >160 bpm.
Baseline Variability	Fluctuations in the baseline FHR are irregular in amplitude and frequency and are visually quantified as the amplitude of the peak to trough in bpm.
– Absent variability	Amplitude range undetectable.
– Minimal variability	Amplitude range visually detectable (>undetectable) but ≤5 bpm.
– Moderate variability	Amplitude range 6–25 bpm.
– Marked variability	Amplitude range >25 bpm.
Acceleration	Visually apparent *abrupt* increase (onset to peak is <30 seconds) in FHR above the adjacent baseline. The FHR peak is ≥15 bpm above the baseline and lasts ≥15 seconds but <2 minutes from the onset to return to baseline. Before 32 weeks of gestation, a peak ≥10 bpm above the baseline and duration of ≥10 seconds is an acceleration.
Prolonged Acceleration	Acceleration ≥2 minutes but <10 minutes duration.
Early Deceleration	Visually apparent, usually symmetrical *gradual* decrease (onset to nadir is ≥30 seconds) of the FHR and return to baseline associated with a uterine contraction. This decrease in FHR is calculated from the onset to the nadir of the deceleration. The nadir of deceleration occurs at the same time as the peak of the contraction. In most cases, the onset, nadir and recovery of the deceleration are coincident with the beginning, peak and ending of the contraction, respectively.

(continued)

Term	Definition
Late Deceleration	Visually apparent, usually symmetrical *gradual* decrease (onset to nadir is ≥30 seconds) of the FHR and return to baseline associated with a uterine contraction. This decrease is calculated from the onset to the nadir of the deceleration. It is delayed in timing, with the nadir of deceleration occurring after the peak of the contraction. In most cases, the onset, nadir and recovery of the deceleration occur after the onset, peak and ending of the contraction, respectively.
Variable Deceleration	Visually apparent *abrupt* decrease (onset to beginning of nadir is <30 seconds) in FHR below baseline. The decrease is calculated from the onset to the nadir of the deceleration. Decrease is 15 bpm, lasting ≥15 seconds but <2 minutes in duration. When variable decelerations are associated with uterine contractions, their onset, depth and duration vary with successive uterine contractions.
Prolonged Deceleration	Visually apparent decrease in FHR below baseline. Decrease is ≥15 bpm, lasting ≥2 minutes but <10 minutes from onset to return to baseline.
	A deceleration that lasts greater than or equal to 10 minutes is a baseline change.
Recurrent	Occurring with ≥ 50% of contractions in a 20-minute period.
Intermittent	Occurring with <50% of contractions in a 20-minute period.
Sinusoidal	Visually apparent undulating sine wave-like pattern in FHR baseline and cycle frequency of 3–5 per minute which persists for ≥20 minutes.

Macones, G. A., Hankins, G. D., Spong, C. Y., Hauth, J. D., & Moore, T. (2008). The 2008 National Institute of Child Health Human Development workshop report on electronic fetal monitoring: Update on definitions, interpretations, and research guidelines. *Obstetrics & Gynecology, 112*, 661–666; and *Journal of Obstetric, Gynecologic and Neonatal Nursing, 37*, 510–515.

2008 THREE-TIER FETAL HEART RATE INTERPRETATION SYSTEM

Category I
*Category I fetal heart rate (FHR) tracings include **all** of the following:* • Baseline rate: 110–160 beats per minute (bpm) • Baseline FHR variability: moderate • Late or variable decelerations: absent • Early decelerations: present or absent • Accelerations: present or absent

Category II
Category II FHR tracings include all FHR tracings not categorized as Category I or Category III. Category II tracings may represent an appreciable fraction of those encountered in clinical care. Examples of Category II FHR tracings include any of the following: **Baseline Rate** • Bradycardia not accompanied by absent baseline variability • Tachycardia **Baseline FHR Variability** • Minimal baseline variability • Absent baseline variability not accompanied by recurrent decelerations • Marked baseline variability **Accelerations** • Absence of induced accelerations after fetal stimulation **Periodic or Episodic Decelerations** • Recurrent variable decelerations accompanied by minimal or moderate baseline variability • Prolonged deceleration ≥2 minutes but <10 minutes • Recurrent late decelerations with moderate baseline variability • Variable decelerations with other characteristics, such as slow return to baseline, "overshoots," or "shoulders"

Category III

Category III FHR tracings include either
 	
• Absent baseline FHR variability and any of the following:
  - Recurrent late decelerations
  - Recurrent variable decelerations
  - Bradycardia
• Sinusoidal pattern

Note: From: The 2008 National Institute of Child Health Human Development Workshop report on electronic fetal monitoring: Update on definitions, interpretations, and research guidelines, by G. A. Macones, G. D. Hankins, C. Y. Spong, J. D. Hauth, & T. Moore, 2008, *Journal of Obstetric, Gynecologic and Neonatal Nursing,* 37, 510–515; *Obstetrics & Gynecology,* 112, p. 665. Copyright 2008 by the American College of Obstetricians and Gynecologists. Reprinted with permission.

REFERENCES

Introduction and Physiology

American Academy of Pediatrics and American College of Obstetricians and Gynecologists. (2012). *Guidelines for perinatal care* (7th ed., pp. 169–210). Elk Grove Village, IL: Authors.

American College of Obstetricians and Gynecologists. (2009). *Intrapartum fetal heart rate monitoring: Nomenclature, interpretation and general management principles* (Practice bulletin number 106). Washington, DC: Author.

American College of Obstetricians and Gynecologists. (2014). Practice bulletin number 145. Antepartum fetal surveillance. Washington, DC: Author.

American College of Obstetricians and Gynecologists. (2014). Committee opinion number 611 Method for Estimating Due Date. http://www.acog.org/Resources-And-Publications/Committee-Opinions/Committee-on-Obstetric-Practice/Method-for-Estimating-Due-Date.

American College of Obstetricians and Gynecologists. (2013). Obesity in Pregnancy. Committee opinion number 549, 1–5.

http://www.cdc.gov/nchs/data/nvsr/nvsr64/nvsr64_05.pdf

Institute of Medicine. (2009). Weight gain during pregnancy: Reexamining the guidelines. Washington DC: National Academies Press.

Larsen, L. G., Clausen, H. V., & Jonsson, L. (2002). Stereologic examination of placentas from mothers who smoke during pregnancy. *American Journal of Obstetrics & Gynecology, 186,* 531–537.

Lyndon, A. & Ali, L. (Eds.). (2015). *Fetal heart monitoring principles and practices* (5th ed.). Dubuque, IA: Kendall Hunt Publishing.

Macones, G.A., Hankins, G.D., Spong, C.Y., Hauth, J.D., & Moore, T. (2008). The 2008 National Institute of Child Health and Human Development workshop report on electronic fetal monitoring: Update on definitions, interpretations, and research guidelines. *Obstetrics & Gynecology, 112,* 661–666; and *Journal of Obstetric, Gynecologic & Neonatal Nursing, 37,* 510–515.

National Institute of Child Health and Human Development Research Planning Workshop. (1997). Electronic fetal heart rate monitoring: Research guidelines for interpretation. *Journal of Obstetric, Gynecologic & Neonatal Nursing, 26,* 635–640 and *American Journal of Obstetrics & Gynecology, 177,* 1385–1390.

The Institute of Medicine. (2003). *Health professions education: A bridge to quality.* Washington, DC: National Academies Press.

The Joint Commission on Accreditation of Healthcare Organizations (The Joint Commission). (2004). Preventing infant death during delivery (Sentinel Event Alert number 30).

http://www.jointcommission.org/sentinel_event_alert_issue_30_preventing_infant_death_and_injury_during_delivery/ (retrieved December 11, 2015).

Interpretation

American College of Obstetricians and Gynecologists. (2013). Executive Summary: *Hypertension in Pregnancy. American Journal of Obstetrics & Gynecology,* 5, 122. http://www.acog.org/Womens-Health/Preeclampsia-and-Hypertension-in-Pregnancy.

American College of Obstetricians and Gynecologists. (2012). Committee opinion number 545: Non-invasive prenatal testing for fetal aneuploidy. Washington, DC: Author. http://www.acog.org/Resources-And-Publications/Committee-Opinions/Committee-on-Genetics/Noninvasive-Prenatal-Testing-for-Fetal-Aneuploidy. http://www.acog.org/Resources-And-Publications/Committee-Opinions/Committee-on-Genetics/Cell-free-DNA-Screening-for-Fetal-Aneuploidy.

American College of Obstetricians and Gynecologists. (2009). Intrapartum fetal heart rate monitoring: Nomenclature, interpretation and general management principles (Practice bulletin number 106). Washington, DC: Author.

American College of Obstetricians and Gynecologists. (2014). Practice bulletin number 145, Antepartum fetal surveillance. Washington, DC: Author.

American College of Obstetrics and Gynecology. (2014). Practice bulletin number 146: Management of late-term and post-term pregnancies. Washington, DC: Author.

American College of Obstetrics and Gynecology. (2002). Practice bulletin number 33, Diagnosis and management of preeclampsia and eclampsia. Washington, DC: Author.

Andres, R., Saade, G., Gilstrap, L., Wilkins, I., Witlin, A., Zlatnik, F., et al. (1999). Association between umbilical blood gas parameters and neonatal morbidity and death in neonates with pathologic fetal acidemia. *American Journal of Obstetrics and Gynecology, 181,* 867–871.

Association of Women's Health, Obstetric and Neonatal Nurses. (2008). *Nursing care and management of the second stage of labor; evidence based clinical practice guideline* (2nd ed.). Washington, DC: Author.

Bakker, P. C. A. M., Kurver, P. H. J., Kuik, D. J., Van Geijn, H. P. (2007). Elevated uterine activity increases the risk of fetal acidosis at birth. *American Journal of Obstetrics and Gynecology 196*(4): 313e1–313e6.

Bakker P. C. A. M & Van Geijn, H. P. (2008). Uterine activity: Implications for the condition of the fetus. *Journal of Perinatal Medicine 36,* 30–37.

Ball, R., & Parer, J. (1992). The physiologic mechanisms of variable decelerations. *American Journal of Obstetrics and Gynecology, 166,* 1683–1688.

Caldeyro-Barcia, R., & Poseiro, J. (1960). Physiology of uterine contractions. *Clinical Obstetrics and Gynecology, 3,* 386–408.

Clark S., Cotton, D., Pivarnik, J., Lee, W., Hankins, G., Benedetti, T., & Phelan, J. (1991). Position change and central hemodynamic profile during normal third-trimester pregnancy and postpartum. *American Journal of Obstetrics and Gynecology, 164*(3), 883–887.

Clark, S. , Nageotte, M., Garite, T., Freeman, R., Miller, D., Simpson, K., et al. (2013). Intrapartum management of category II fetal heart rate tracings: Towards standardization of care. *American Journal of Obstetrics and Gynecology 209*(2), 89–97.

Clark, S., Simpson, K., Knox, G., & Garite, T. (2009). Oxytocin: New perspectives on an old drug. *American Journal of Obstetrics and Gynecology 200,* 35.e1–35.e6.

Cochrane Database of Systematic Reviews. (2012). Maternal oxygen administration for fetal distress.

Crane, J. & Young, D. (1998). Meta-analysis of low-dose versus high-dose oxytocin for labour induction. *Journal of the Society of Obstetricians and Gynaecologists of Canada, 20,* 1215–1223.Rubin, E. (1915). *Synsoplevede figurer* (vol. 1). Gylendhal.

Elliott, C., Warrick, P. A., Graham, E., & Hamilton, E. F. (2010). Graded classification of fetal heart rate tracings: Association with neonatal metabolic acidosis and neurologic morbidity. *American Journal of Obstetrics and Gynecology, 202*(3), 258. E1–258.E 8.

Fox, M., Kilpatrick, S., King, T., & Parer, J. T. (2000). Fetal heart rate monitoring: Interpretation and collaborative management. *Journal of Nurse Midwifery and Women's Health, 45,* 498–507.

Freeman, R., Garite, T., & Nageotte, M. (1991). *Fetal heart rate monitoring* (2nd ed., p. 17). Baltimore: Williams & Wilkins.

Freeman, R., Garite, T., Nageotte, M., & Miller, L. (2012). *Fetal heart rate monitoring* (4th ed., p. 134). Philadelphia, PA: Lippincott Williams & Wilkins.

Frey, H., Tuuli, M., Cortez, S., Odibo, A., Roehl, K., Shanks, A., Macones, G., & Cahil, A. (2012). Does delayed pushing in the second stage of labor impact perinatal outcomes. *American Journal of Perinatology, 29*(10), 807–814.

Gilstrap, L. (2004). Fetal acid-base balance. In R. Creasy, R. Resnick, & J. Iams (Eds.). *Maternal-fetal medicine: Principles and practice* (5th ed., p. 434). Philadelphia : W.B. Saunders Company.

Hamilton, E., Warrick, P., Knox, E., O'Keeffe, D., & Garite, T. (2012). High uterine contraction rates in births with normal and abnormal umbilical artery gases. *Journal of Maternal Fetal & Neonatal Medicine, 25*(11), 2302–2307.

Hamel, M. S., Anderson, B. L., & Rouse, D. J. (2014). Oxygen for intrauterine resuscitation: Of unproved benefit and potentially harmful. *American Journal of Obstetrics & Gynecology, 211*, 124–127.

Hauth, J., Hankins, G., Gilstrap, L., Strickland, D., & Vance, P. (1986). Oxytocin and contractility of the pregnant human uterus. Oxytocin augmentation of dysfunctional labor. II. Uterine activity data. *Obstetrics & Gynecology, 68*(3), 305.

Jackson, M., Holmgren, C. M., Esplin, M. S., Henry, E., & Varner, M. W. (2011). Frequency of fetal heart rate categories and short-term neonatal outcome. *Obstetrics & Gynecology, 118*(4), 803–808.

Klauser, C. K., Christensen, E. E., Chauhan, S. P., Bufkin, L., Magann, E., & Bofill, J. (2005). Use of fetal pulse oximetry among high-risk women in labor: A randomized clinical trial. *American Journal of Obstetrics and Gynecology, 192*(16), 1810–1819.

Low, J., Lindsay, B., & Derrickm, J. (1997). Threshold of metabolic acidosis associated with newborn complications. *American Journal of Obstetrics and Gynecology, 177*, 1391–1394.

Lyndon, A. & Ali, L. (2015). *Fetal heart monitoring principles and practices* (5th ed.). Dubuque, IA: Kendall Hunt Publishing.

Macones, G. A., Hankins, G. D., Spong, C. Y., Hauth, J. D., & Moore, T. (2008). The 2008 National Institute of Child Health and Human Development workshop report on electronic fetal monitoring: Update on definitions, interpretations, and research guidelines. *Obstetrics & Gynecology, 112*, 661–666; and *Journal of Obstetric, Gynecologic & Neonatal Nursing, 37,* 510–515.

Miller, L., Miller, D., & Tucker, S. (2013). *Mosby's pocket guide to fetal monitoring: A multidisciplinary approach* (7th ed., pp. 127–128). New York: Elsevier.

National High Blood Pressure Education Program Working Group, 2000.

Parer, J. (1997). *Handbook of fetal heart rate monitoring* (2nd ed., p. 224). Philadelphia: W.B. Saunders Company.

Rinehart, B. K., Terrone, D. A., Barrow, J. H., Isler, C. M., Barrilleaux, P. S., & Roberts, W. E. (2000). Randomized trial of intermittent or continuous amnioinfusion for variable decelerations. *Obstetrics & Gynecology, 96*(4), 571–574.

Schulman, H., & Romney, S. (1970). A quantitative study of the action of synthetic oxytocin on the pregnant human uterus. *Obstetrics& Gynecology 36* (2):215–221.

Seitchik, J., & Castillo, M. (1983). Variability of uterine contractions in normal human parturition. *American Journal of Obstetrics & Gynecology 145*(5), 526.

Simpson, K. R. & James, D. C. (2005). Efficacy of intrauterine resuscitation techniques in improving fetal oxygen status during labor. *Obstetrics & Gynecology, 105,* 1362–1368.

Simpson, K. R. (2008). Intrauterine resuscitation during labor: Should maternal oxygen administration be a first-line measure? *Seminars in Fetal & Neonatal Medicine, 13,* 362–367.

Techniques

American College of Nurse Midwives. (2010). Intermittent auscultation for intrapartum fetal heart rate surveillance. *Journal of Midwifery and Women's Health, 55*(4), 397–403.

American College of Obstetricians and Gynecologists. (2003). Dystocia and augmentation of labor. Practice Bulletin number 49. Washington, DC: Author.

Association of Women's Health, Obstetric and Neonatal Nurses. (2010). Guidelines for professional registered nurse staffing for perinatal units. Washington, DC.

Association of Women's Health Obstetric and Neonatal Nurses. (2015). Fetal Heart Monitoring Position Statement. Washington, DC: Author.

Bakker, J..J. H., Verhoeven, C. H. M., Janssen, P. F., van Lith, J. M., van Oudgaarden, E. D.,

Bloemenkamp, K. W. M., et al. (2010). Outcomes after internal versus external tocody-namometry for monitoring labor. *New England Journal of Medicine 362*(4), 306–313. doi: 10.1056/NEJMoa0902748.

Caldeyro-Barcia, R. & Poseiro, J. (1959). Oxytocin and contractility of the pregnant human uterus. *Annals of the New York Academy of Sciences, 75*, 813–830.

Caldeyro- Barcia, R. & Poseiro, J. (1960). Physiology of the uterine contraction. *Clinics in Obstetrics & Gynecology 3*, 386.

Kleinman, C. S. & Nehgme, R. A. (2004). Cardiac arrhythmias in the human fetus. *Pediatric Cardiology, 25*(3), 234–251.

LaCroix, G. E. (1968). Monitoring labor by an external tocodynamometer. *American Journal of Obstetrics & Gynecology, 101* (1), 111–119.

Neilson, D. R., Freeman, R. K., & Mangan, S. (2008). Signal Ambiguity resulting in unexpected outcomes with external fetal heart rate monitoring. *American Journal of Obstetrics & Gynecology, 198*(6), 717–724.

Paquette, S., Moretti, F., O'Reilly, K., Ferraro, Z., & Oppenheimer, L. (2014). The incidence of maternal artifact during intrapartum fetal heart rate monitoring. *Journal of Obstetrics & Gynecology, 36*(11), 962–968.

Parer, J.T. (1997). *Handbook of fetal heart rate monitoring* (2nd ed.). Philadelphia, PA: WB Saunders.

Sherman, D. J., Frenkel, E., Kurzweil, Y., Padua, A., Arieli, S., & Bahar, M. (2002). Characteristics of maternal heart rate patterns during labor and delivery. *Obstetrics & Gynecology, 99*, 542–547.

Choosing Physiologically Based Interventions

American College of Obstetricians and Gynecologists. (2015). Practice bulletin number 107, Induction of labor. Washington, DC: Author.

American College of Obstetricians and Gynecologists. (2003). Practice bulletin number 49, Dystocia and the augmentation of labor. Washington, DC: Author.

Bakker, P. & Van Geign, H. (2008). Uterine Activity: Implications for the condition of the fetus. *Journal of Perinatal Medicine 36*, 3–-37.

Caldeyro-Barcia, R. & Poseiro, J. (1960). Physiology of uterine contractions. *Clinical Obstetrics & Gynecology, 3*, 386–408.

Centers for Disease Control and Prevention (CDC). (2014). Recent declines in induction of labor by gestational age. NCHS Data Brief No. 155.

Clark, S., Cotton, D., Pivarnik, J. Lee, W., Hankins, G., Benedetti, T., et al. (1991). Position change and central hemodynamic profile during normal third-trimester pregnancy and postpartum. *American Journal of Obstetrics and Gynecology, 164*(3), 883–887.

Clark, S., Simpson, K., Knox, G., & Garite, T. (2009). Oxytocin: New perspectives on an old drug. *American Journal of Obstetrics & Gynecology 200*, 35.e1–35e.6.

Cochrane Database of Systematic Reviews. Maternal oxygen administration for fetal distress, December 12, 2012.

Crane, J. & Young, D. (1998). Meta-analysis of low-dose versus high-dose oxytocin for labour induction. *Journal of the Society of Obstetricians & Gynaecologists of Canada, 20*, 1215–1223.

Daniel-Spiegel, E., Weiner, Z., Ben-Shlomo, I., & Shalev, E (2004). For how long should oxytocin be continued during labor? *BJOG: An International Journal of Obstetrics & Gynecology, 111*, 331–334.

Direkvand-Maghadam, A. & Rezaeian, M. (2012). Increased intravenous hydration of nulliparas in labors. *International Journal of Gynecology and Obstetrics 118*, 213–215.

Elliott, C., Warrick, P. A., Graham, E. & Hamilton, E. F. (2010). Graded classification of fetal heart rate tracings: association with neonatal metabolic acidosis and neurologic morbidity. *American Journal of Obstetrics & Gynecology, 202*(3), 258.e1–258.e8.

Eslamian, L., Marsoosi, V., & Pakneeyat, Y. (2006). Increased intravenous fluid intake and the course of labor in nulliparous women. *International Journal of Gynecology and Obstetrics, 93*, 102–105.

Freeman, R. K., Garite, T. J., Nageotte, M. P., & Miller, L. A. (2012). *Fetal heart rate monitoring* (4th ed., p. 134). Philadelphia PA: Lippincott Williams & Wilkins.

Frey, H., Tuuli, M., Cortez, S., Odibo, A., Roehl, K., Shanks, A., et al. (2012). Does delayed pushing in the second stage of labor impact perinatal outcomes. *American Journal of Perinatology, 29*(10), 807–814.

Garite, T., Weeks, J., Peters-Phan, K., Pattillo, C., & Brewster, W. (2000). A randomized controlled trial of the effect of increased intravenous hydration on the course of labor in nulliparous women. *American Journal of Obstetrics & Gynecology, 183*, 1544–1548.

Hamilton, E., Warrick, P., Knox, E., O'Keefe, D., & Garite, T. (2012). High uterine contraction rates in births with normal and abnormal umbilical artery gases. *Journal of Maternal Fetal Neonatal Medicine, 25*(11), 2302–2307.

Hansen, S., Clark, S., & Foster, J. (2002). Active pushing v. passive descent in the second stage of labor: a randomized controlled trial. *Obstetrics & Gynecology, 99*(1), 29–34.

http://mail.ny.acog.org/website/EFM/ElevatedUterine.pdf

http://www.ctgutbildning.se/Course/referenser/referenser/Bakker%20et%20al%20 2008_2.pdf

http://www.jwatch.org/wh200806190000001/2008/06/19/oxytocin-induced-labor-effects-fetal-oxygen

Jackson, M., Holgren, C., Esplin, M., Henry, E., & Varner, M. (2011). Frequency of fetal heart rate categories and short-term neonatal outcome. *Obstetrics & Gynecology 118*(4), 803–808.

Phaneuf, S., Rodriguez, B., Linares, R., TambyRaja, I., Mackenzie, I., & Lopez Bernal, A. (2000). Loss of myometrial oxytocin receptors during oxytocin-induced and oxytocin-augmented labour. *Journal of Reproduction and Fertility, 120*, 91–97.

Piquard, F., Hsiung, R., Mettauer, M., Shaeffer, A., Haberley, P., & Dellenbach, P. (1988). The validity of fetal heart rate monitoring during the second stage. *Obstetrics & Gynecology, 72*(5), 746–751.

Satin, A., Leveno, K., Sherman, M., & McIintire, D. (1992). Factors affecting the dose response to oxytocin for labor stimulation. *American Journal of Obstetrics & Gynecology, 166*, 1260–1261.

Seitchik, J., Amico, J., Robinson, A. G. A., Castillo, M. (1984). Oxytocin augmentation of dysfunction labor. IV. Oxytocin pharmacokinetics. *American Journal of Obstetrics & Gynecology, 150*, 225–228.

Simpson, K. R. & James, D. C. (2005). Effects of immediate v. delayed pushing during second-stage labor on fetal well-being: A randomized clinical trial. *Nursing Research 54*(3), 149–157.

Simpson, K. R. & James, D. C. (2008). Effects of oxytocin-induced uterine hyperstimulation during labor on fetal oxygen status and fetal heart rate patterns. *American Journal of Obstetrics & Gynecology, 199*, 34e1–34e5.

Simpson, K. R. & James, D. C. (2005). Efficacy of intrauterine resuscitation techniques in improving fetal oxygen status during labor. *Obstetrics & Gynecology, 105*, 1362–1368.

Simpson, K. R. & Knox, E. (2009). Oxytocin as a high-alert medication: Implications for patient safety. *Maternal Child Nursing, 34*, 8–15.

Simpson, K. R. & O'Brien-Abel, N. (2013). Labor and birth. In K. R. Simpson & P. A. Creehan (Eds.). AWHONN's Perinatal Nursing (4th ed., pp. 343–344). Philadelphia, PA: Lippincott Williams & Wilkins.

Communication

Abraham, J., Kannampallil, T. G., & Patel, V. L. (2012). Bridging gaps in handoff: A continuity of care based approach. *Journal of Biomedical Informatics, 45*(2), 240–254. doi:10.1016/j.jbi.2011.10.011.

American College of Obstetricians and Gynecologists. (2011). Committee Opinion number 508. Disruptive behavior. *Obstetrics & Gyncecology, 118*(4), 970–972. doi: 10.1097/AOG.0b013e3182358acc.

American College of Obstetricians and Gynecologists. (2012). Committee Opinion Number 517. Communication strategies for patient handoffs. *Obstetrics & Gynecology, 119*(2, Pt.1), 408–411. doi: 10.1097/AOG.0b013e318249ff4f.

Barker, J. (2009). Improving your safety culture: Learning a lesson from the aviation industry. *Mach One Leadership 2* (2).

Block, M., Ehrenworth, J., Cuce, V., Ng'ang'a, N., Weinback, J., Saber, S., Schleisinger, M. (2010). Tangible handoff: A team approach for advanced structured communication in labor and delivery. *Joint Commission Journal on Quality & Patient Safety, 36*, 282–287, 241.

Garder, R. (2006). Obstetrics-related risk. Forum 8.

Harper, L. M., Shankds, A. L., Tuuli, M. G., Roehl, K. A., & Cahill, A. G. (2013). The risks and benefits of internal monitors in laboring patients. *American Journal of Obstetrics and Gynecology, 209*(1), 38.e1–38.e38.

Leonard, M. W. (2013). SBAR technique for communication: A situational briefing model. Retrieved from http://www.ihi.org/knowledge/Pages/Tools/SBARTechnique forCommunicatonA SituationalBriefingModel.aspx

Leonard, M. W. & Frankel, A. S. (2011). Role of effective teamwork and communication in delivering safe, high-quality care. *Mount Sinai Journal of Medicine, 78*(6), 820–826.

Lyndon, A., Zlatnik, M. G., Masfield, D. G., Lewis, A., McMillan, C., & Kennedy, H. P. (2014). Contributions of clinical disconnections and unresolved conflict to failures in intrapartum safety. *Journal of Obstetric, Gynecologic and Neonatal Nursing, 43*(1), 2–12. doi:10.1111.1552-6909.12266.

Ong, M. S. & Coiera, E. (2011). A systematic review of failures in handoff communication during intrahospital transfers. *Joint Commission Journal on Quality and Patient Safety, 37*(6), 274–284.

Riesenberg, L. A., Leitzsch, J., & Cunningham, J. M. (2010). Nursing Handoff: A systematic review of the literature. *American Journal of Nursing, 110*(4), 24–34.

Simpson, K. R. (2014). Perinatal patient safety and professional liability issues. In K. R. Simpson & P. A.

Creehan (Eds.). *Perinatal nursing* (4th ed., pp. 1–40). Philadelphia, PA: Lippincott Williams & Wilkins.

Shostek, K. & Clark, C. (2008). Communication plays key role in OB patient expectations. *Journal of Healthcare Risk Management, 28*(4), 29–32.

The Joint Commission. (2008). Behaviors that undermine a culture of safety. *Sentinel Event Alert* (40)103. (http://www.jointcommission.org/assets/1/18/SEA_40.PDF)

White, A. A., Pichert, J. E., Bledsoe, S. H., Irin, C., & Entman, S. S. (2005). Cause and effect analysis of closed claims in obstetrics and gynecology. *Obstetrics & Gynecology, 105*, 1031–1038.

Wilson-Stronks, A., Lee K. K., Cordero, C. L., Kopp, A. L., & Galvez, E. (2008). One size does not fit all: Meeting the health care needs of diverse populations. Retrieval from http://www.jointcommission.org/assets/1/6/HLCOneSizeFinal.pdf.

AWHONN
PROMOTING THE HEALTH OF
WOMEN AND NEWBORNS

The Association of Women's Health, Obstetric and Neonatal Nurses (AWHONN) is the leading profession-al association committed to promoting the health of women and newborns. AWHONN provides the tools and resources to help you become a great nurse! By joining AWHONN you open the door to a wealth of educational resources and opportunities to help you take the next step in your personal and professional development.

Membership Benefits

- Subscription to *Journal of Obstetric, Gynecologic and Neonatal Nursing* (JOGNN)

- Subscription to *Nursing for Women's Health*

- Access to Free Webinars and Journal CNE through the AWHONN Online Learning Center

- Free member-only tools and resources

- AWHONN's bi-weekly *SmartBrief* email newsletter

- Discounts on Annual Convention Registration

- Networking & Peer Education Opportunities through Local Sections & Chapters

- Professional Development and Leadership Opportunities

- Access to Career Management Tools in the AWHONN Career Center

- Special discounts on Personal Liability & Auto Insurance, Scrubs, Travel, Car Rental, Financial Planning, and more!

Visit www.awhonn.org to join and start taking advantage of your member benefits today!

AWHONN Intermediate Fetal Heart Monitoring Course

1

_____

About AWHONN

The Association of Women's Health, Obstetric and Neonatal Nurses (AWHONN) is the foremost nursing authority promoting the health of women and newborns and strengthening the nursing profession through the delivery of advocacy, research, education and evidence-based clinical resources.

AWHONN represents the interests of 350,000 registered nurses working in women's health, obstetric and neonatal nurses across the United States.

2

_____

Key Activities

- Two Leading Scholarly Journals:
  - ➤ *JOGNN/Nursing for Women's Health*
- Annual Convention
- Fetal Heart Monitoring Program
- Advocacy Work and Research Program
- Evidence-Based Clinical Practice Guidelines
- Webinars and Online Education

3

Course Objectives

- Assess EFM tracings utilizing NICHD terminology
- Interpret EFM tracings, analyze uterine activity, and discuss contractions' impact on fetal oxygenation
- Describe clinical interventions and the related maternal-fetal physiology
- Effectively communicate patient data through verbal and documentation methods
- Describe roles and responsibilities of health care providers when using FHM in intrapartum care

4

Disclosures

- Instructors must disclose conflicts of interest and/or relevant financial relationships
- Instructors must disclose if no conflicts exist.
- The nurse planners for this course report no conflicts of interest or relationships with commercial interest organizations.

5

AWHONN Fetal Monitoring Program

- Overarching goal to provide common foundation of knowledge and skills relating to FHM
- Recognizes that clinicians' knowledge, experiences and skills differ
- Patient safety promoted when all clinicians use standardized terminology

6

2008 NICHD/ACOG EFM Workshop

- Revisited the 1997 report
- Titled "The 2008 National Institute of Child Health and Human Development Workshop Report on Electronic Fetal Monitoring: Update on Definitions, Interpretation, and Research Guidelines"

  – Provides definitions for categorization of FHM tracings

7

Collaborative Fetal Monitoring Process and Evaluation

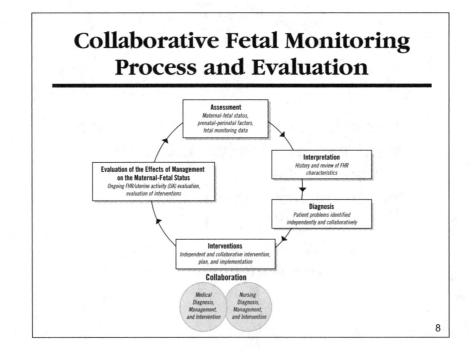

8

Assessment

Maternal and Fetal Data Base

9

Assessment: Maternal–Fetal Data Base

- History
- Family
- Medical/ surgical
- Obstetric
- Psychosocial issues

- Current pregnancy:
  - Maternal assessment:
    - Medical/surgical history
    - Obstetric issues
    - Psychosocial issues

10

Assessment: Maternal–Fetal Data Base

– Fetal assessment:
➤ Gestational age
➤ Fetal activity
➤ FHR

11

_____

_____

_____

_____

Current Pregnancy

▪ Prenatal records:

– Labs

– Weight gain/loss

– Vital sign trends

– Ultrasound reports

– Fundal height trends

12

_____

_____

_____

_____

Current Pregnancy

- Patient interview:
  - Signs of labor
  - Signs of fetal well-being

13

_____

_____

_____

_____

Current Pregnancy

- Abnormal findings that would necessitate prompt communication with a provider

14

_____

_____

_____

_____

Current Pregnancy

- Physical assessment:
  - Maternal vital signs
  - Indicators of maternal-fetal oxygenation
  - Assessment of labor status (maternal)
  - Assessment of maternal and fetal tolerance of labor

15

Extrinsic Influences on Fetal Heart Patterns

- Maternal–fetal exchange:
  - Placenta
  - Maternal utero-placental circulation
  - Fetal-placental circulation
  - Placental transfer
  - Uterine blood flow
  - Umbilical cord
  - Amniotic fluid

16

Extrinsic Influences

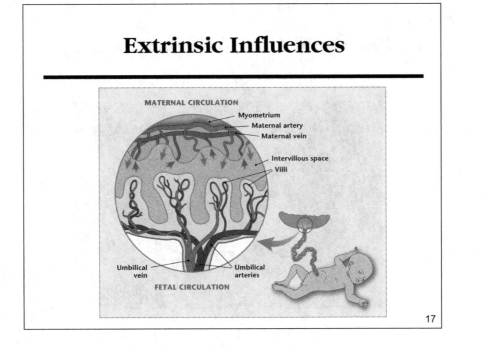

17

Extrinsic Influences

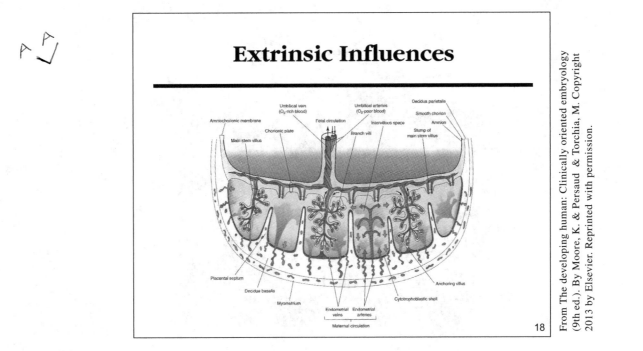

18

From The developing human: Clinically oriented embryology (9th ed.). By Moore, K. & Persaud & Torchia, M. Copyright 2013 by Elsevier. Reprinted with permission.

Placental Calcification: Aging

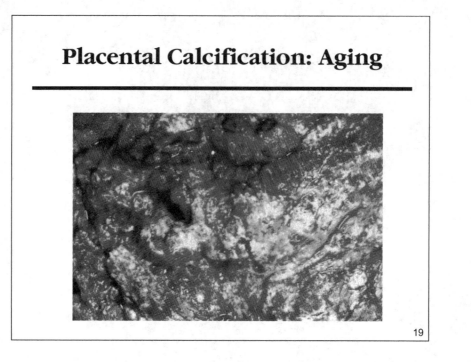

19

Placental Transfer Capacity

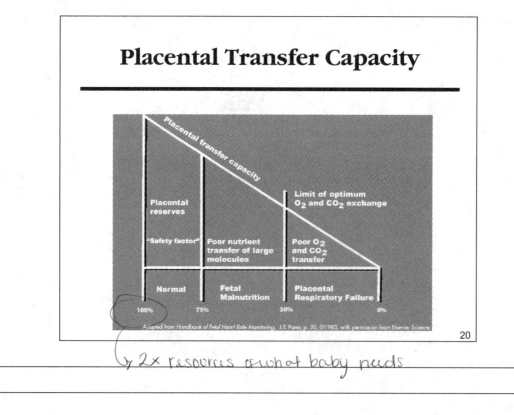

20

↳ 2x resources of what baby needs

Amniotic Fluid Volume (mL)

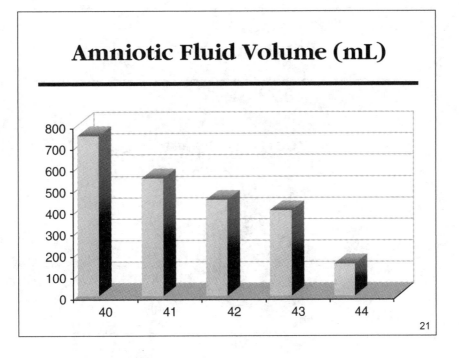

21

Indirect indicator of placental function

Intrinsic Influences on FHR: Fetal Homeostatic Compensatory Mechanisms

- Fetal circulation
- Autonomic nervous system responses
- Baroreceptors
- Chemoreceptors
- Hormonal responses
  ➢ Redistribution of blood flow

22

Fetal Circulation

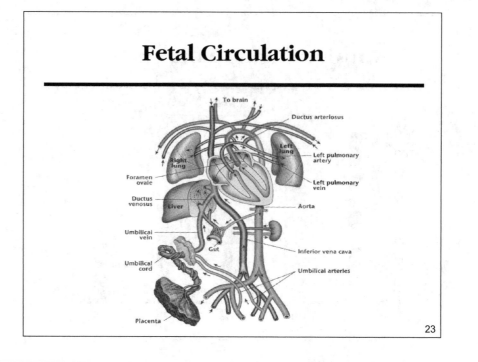

23

Regulation of Fetal Heart Rate and Blood Flow

- Cardio regulatory center (CRC)
- Autonomic nervous system:
  - Parasympathetic
  - Sympathetic
- Baroreceptors
- Chemoreceptors
- Hormonal responses

24

Regulation of Fetal Heart Rate and Blood Flow

- Cardio regulatory center (CRC)
- Autonomic nervous system:
  - Parasympathetic ↑ with ↑ age
  - Sympathetic
- Baroreceptors
- Chemoreceptors
- Hormonal responses

25

↑ GA = ↓ HR + ↑ variability

Intrinsic Influences on FHR

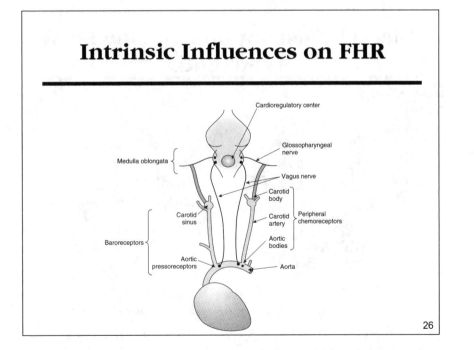

26

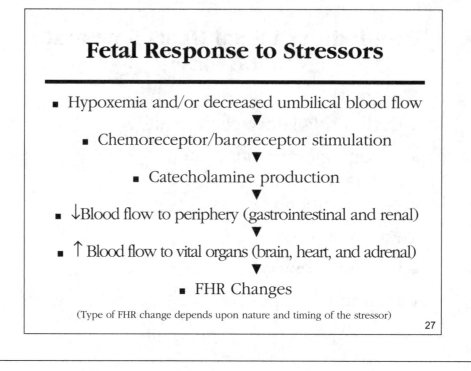

Fetal Response to Stressors

- Hypoxemia and/or decreased umbilical blood flow
  ▼
  - Chemoreceptor/baroreceptor stimulation
    ▼
    - Catecholamine production
      ▼
- ↓Blood flow to periphery (gastrointestinal and renal)
  ▼
- ↑ Blood flow to vital organs (brain, heart, and adrenal)
  ▼
  - FHR Changes

(Type of FHR change depends upon nature and timing of the stressor)

27

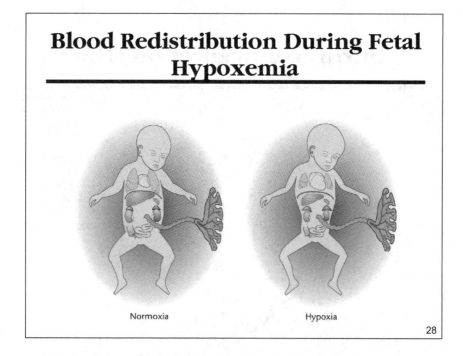

Blood Redistribution During Fetal Hypoxemia

Normoxia   Hypoxia

28

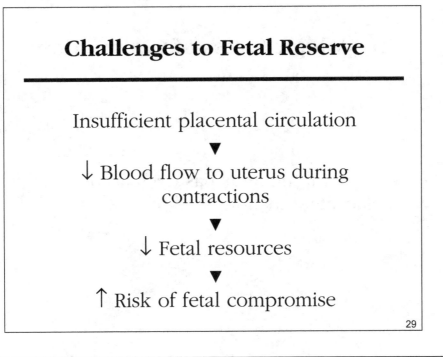

Challenges to Fetal Reserve

Insufficient placental circulation

▼

↓ Blood flow to uterus during contractions

▼

↓ Fetal resources

▼

↑ Risk of fetal compromise

29

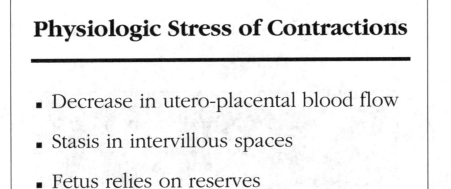

Physiologic Stress of Contractions

- Decrease in utero-placental blood flow

- Stasis in intervillous spaces

- Fetus relies on reserves

30

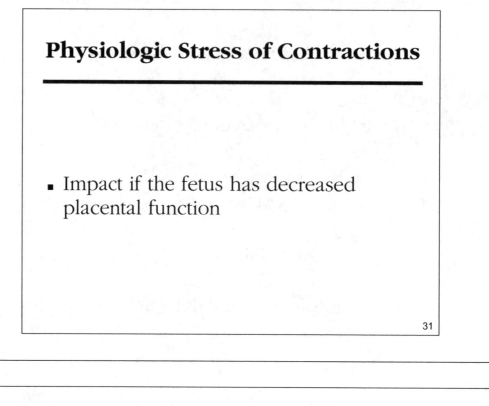

Physiologic Stress of Contractions

- Impact if the fetus has decreased placental function

31

_____

_____

_____

_____

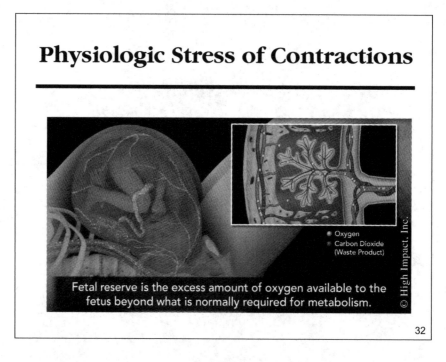

Physiologic Stress of Contractions

Oxygen
Carbon Dioxide
(Waste Product)

Fetal reserve is the excess amount of oxygen available to the
fetus beyond what is normally required for metabolism.

© High Impact, Inc.

32

_____

_____

_____

_____

Fetal Reserve

- The degree of hypoxemia a fetus can tolerate before true tissue hypoxia and acidosis occur.

  – Placental transfer capacity

  – Fetal homeostatic compensatory responses

33

_____

_____

_____

_____

Fetal Reserve

Alterations in compensatory mechanisms.

34

_____

_____

_____

_____

Fetal Well-Being

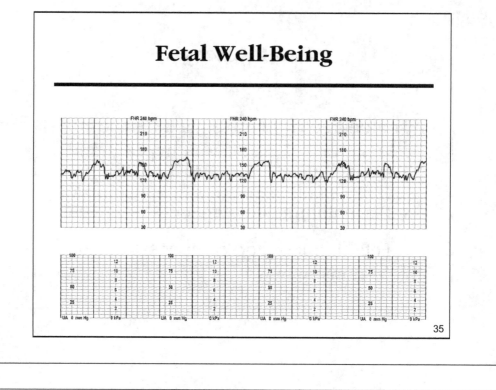

35

Savannah

- Age: 28
- Gravidity/parity: G3P1102
- Gestational age: 41 weeks
- Medical history: obesity
- Surgical history: unremarkable
- Psychosocial history: works in retail, unmarried, but FOB involved, smokes 1/2 pack per day

36

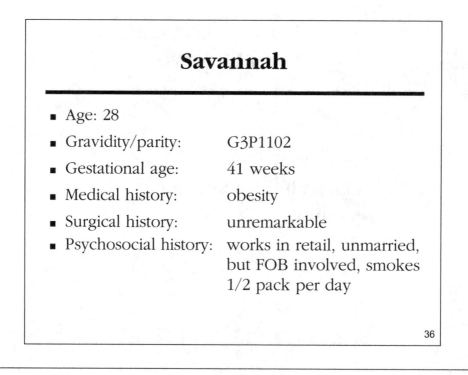

Savannah

- Past OB history: SVD at 40 3/7 weeks
                      SVD at 35 weeks

- Current OB history: FGR

37

Savannah

- VE: 3 cm/80%/-1
  - Vertex presentation
  - Intact membranes

- VS:
  - T: 98.3°F (36.8°C)
  - BP: 136/72
  - HR: 84 bpm
  - RR: 20/min.

38

Savannah

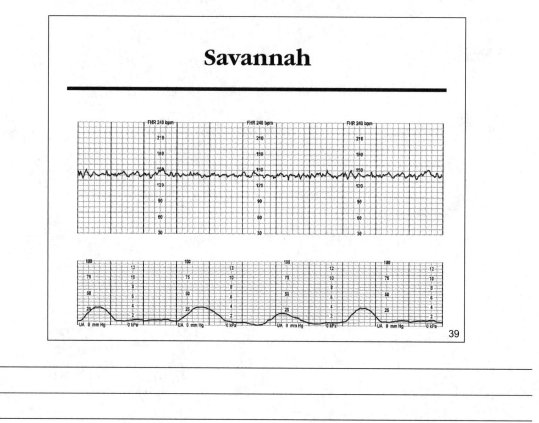

Savannah: 2 Hours Later

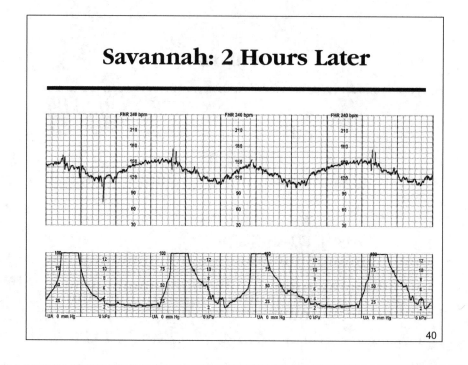

Savannah: 2 Hours Later

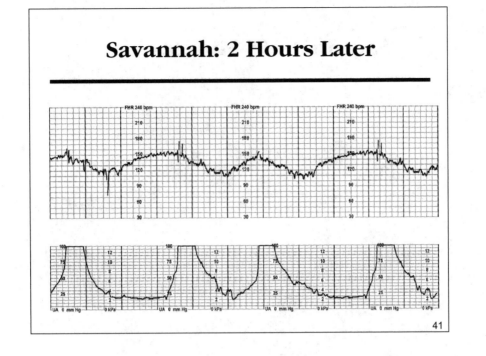

41

Savannah: 45 Minutes Later

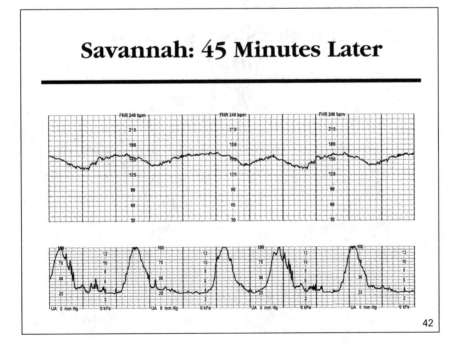

42

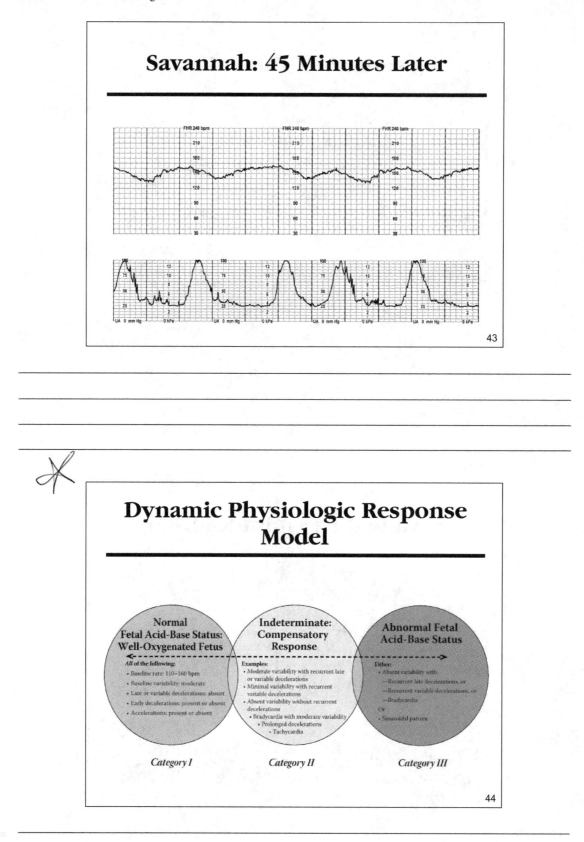

Maternal–Fetal Database

- Risk factors:
  - History
  - Current pregnancy
- Physiologic significance
- Implications for fetal well-being/ oxygenation

45

Maternal and Fetal Physical Assessment

- Maternal vital signs and physical exam
- Fetal presentation
- Fetal movement
- Fetal heart assessment
- Uterine activity
- Labor progress

46

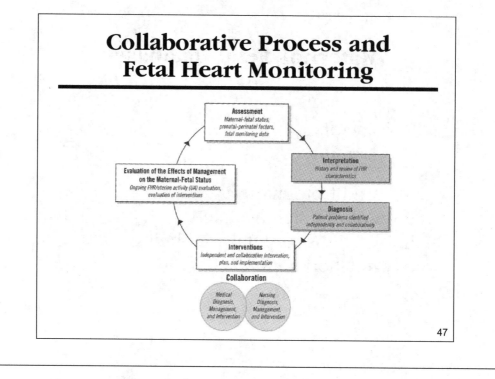

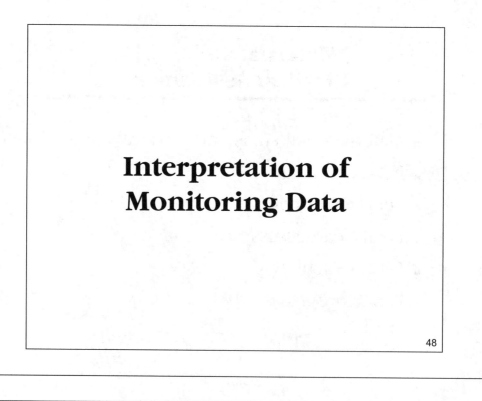

Exercise

Edgar Rubin titled Synsoplevede Figurer, volume 1 published by Gyldendal in 1915

49

_____

_____

_____

_____

Systematic Assessment of Monitor Tracings

- Baseline rate
- Variability
- Periodic/episodic changes
- Uterine activity
  – Frequency, duration, intensity and resting tone

50

_____

_____

_____

_____

Systematic Assessment of Monitor Tracings

- Pattern evolution
- Accompanying clinical characteristics

51

Systematic Assessment of Monitor Tracings

- Potential need for communication with the provider and/or to carry out bedside interventions

52

Baseline Fetal Heart Rate

The approximate mean FHR rounded to increments of 5 bpm during a 10-minute window, excluding:

- Accelerations and decelerations
- Periods of marked variability (>25 bpm)

There must be at least 2 minutes of identifiable baseline segments (not necessarily contiguous) in a 10-minute window, or the baseline for that period is indeterminate.

–Macones et al. (2008)

53

Baseline Fetal Heart Rate

Normal range: 110–160 bpm

Bradycardia: a baseline of <110 bpm for ≥ 10 minutes

Tachycardia: a baseline of >160 bpm for ≥ 10 minutes

–Macones et al. (2008)

54

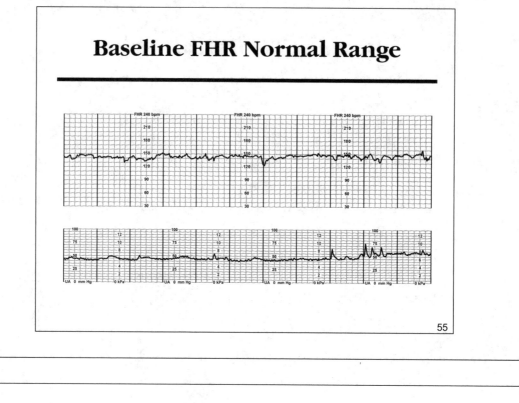

Baseline FHR Normal Range

55

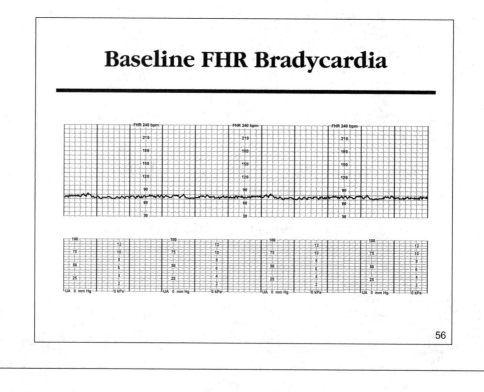

Baseline FHR Bradycardia

56

Baseline FHR Tachycardia

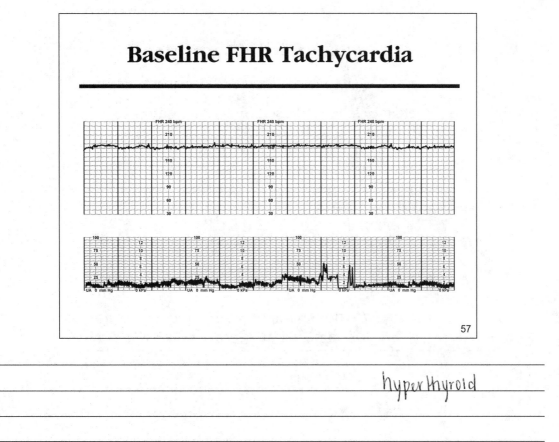

57

hyper thyroid

Sinusoidal FHR

fetal anemia - abruption   20min

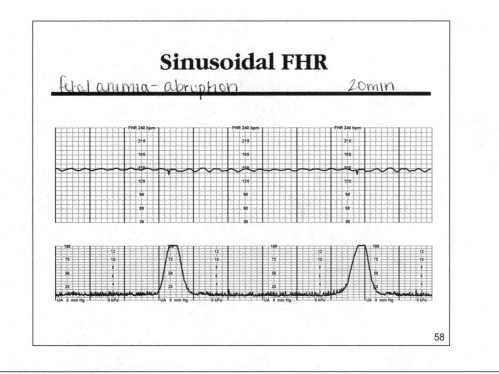

58

Baseline FHR Variability

- Fluctuations in the baseline FHR that are irregular in amplitude and frequency
- Quantified as the amplitude of the peak-to-trough in bpm
- Amplitude range is visually quantified as follows:
  - ➤ *Absent* FHR variability = Undetectable amplitude range
  - ➤ *Minimal* FHR variability = > undetectable ≤5 bpm
  - ➤ *Moderate* FHR variability = 6–25 bpm amplitude range
  - ➤ *Marked* FHR variability = ≥25 bpm amplitude
    -Macones et al. (2008)

59

FHR Variability

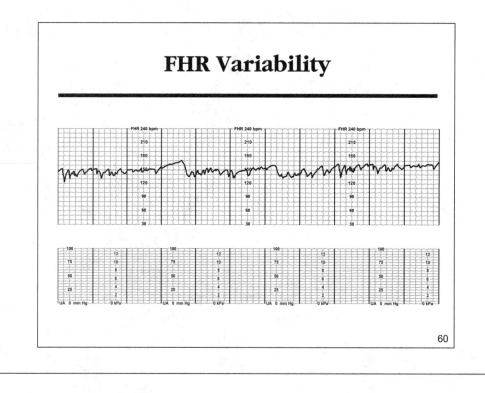

60

Absent FHR Variability

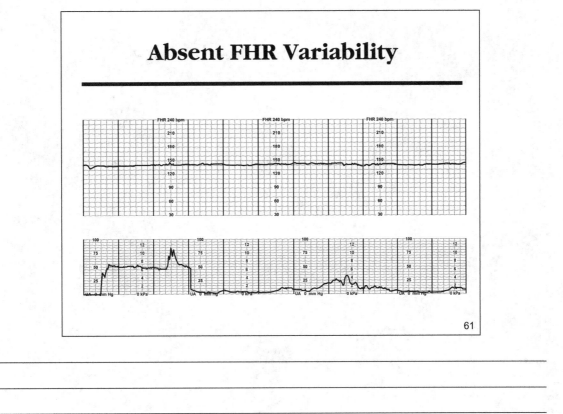

61

Sleep cycle – 20–60min

Minimal FHR Variability

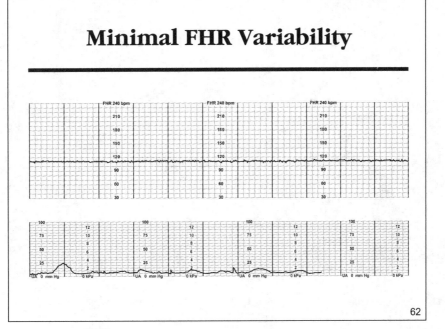

62

Moderate FHR Variability

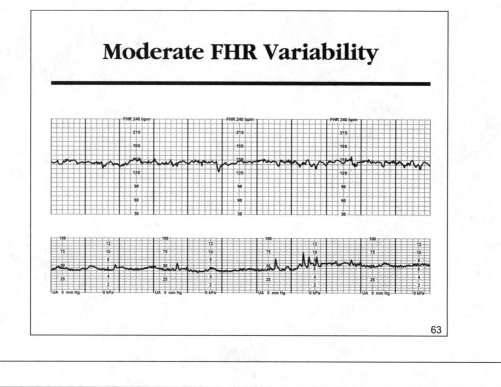

63

Marked FHR Variability

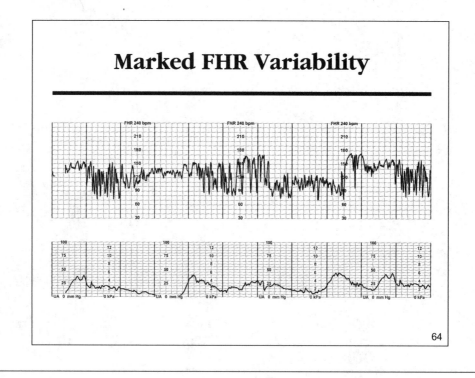

64

FHR Variability?

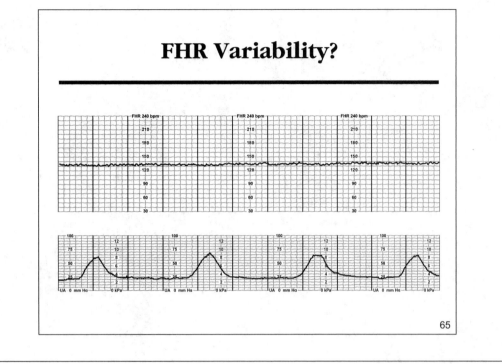

65

FHR Variability?

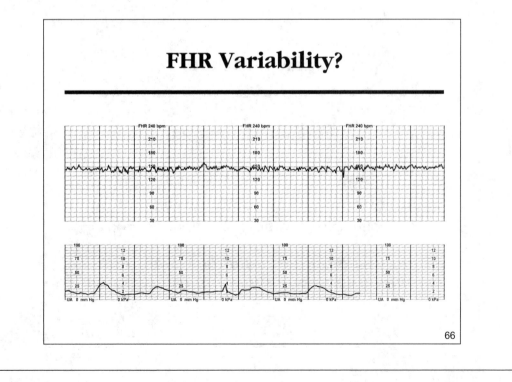

66

FHR Variability?

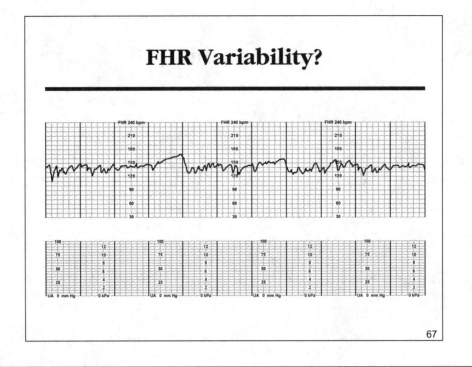

67

FHR Patterns

Periodic: associated with uterine contractions

Episodic: not associated with uterine contractions

Recurrent: decelerations that occur with ≥50% of uterine contractions within a 20-minute period

Intermittent: decelerations that occur with <50% of uterine contractions within a 20-minute period

–Macones et al. (2008)   68

FHR Accelerations

- Visually apparent abrupt (onset to peak in <30 seconds) increases in FHR above the baseline
- In fetus ≥32 weeks, peak ≥15 bpm and last for ≥15 seconds from onset to return to baseline
- In fetus <32 weeks, peak ≥10 bpm and last for ≥10 seconds from onset to return to baseline
- *Prolonged* acceleration is ≥2 minutes but <10 minutes in duration
- Indicate normal fetal acid-base status

–Macones et al. (2008)

69

FHR Accelerations

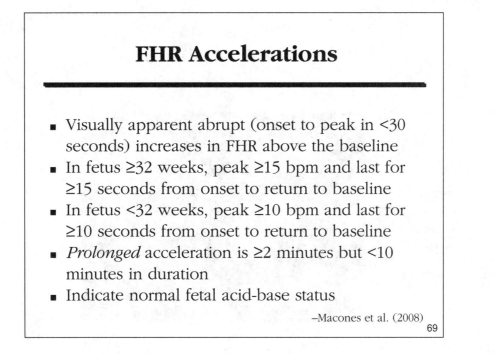

70

FHR Decelerations

Type	Definition: Visually apparent decrease in FHR
Early	*Gradual* onset: ≥ 30 sec from onset to nadir; nadir simultaneous with peak of contraction
Late	*Gradual* onset: ≥ 30 sec from onset to nadir; delayed in timing – nadir after peak of contraction
Variable	*Abrupt* onset: < 30 sec from onset to beginning of nadir, lasting ≥ 15 sec but < 2 min.; depth ≥ 15 bpm
Prolonged	Decrease of ≥ 15 bpm lasting ≥ 2 minutes but less than 10 minutes (≥ 10 min. = baseline change)

71

Periodic vs. Episodic FHR Patterns

- *Periodic*: associated with uterine contractions

- *Episodic*: not associated with uterine contractions

72

Recurrent vs. Intermittent Patterns

- *Recurrent*: decelerations that occur with ≥50% of uterine contractions within a 20-minute period.

- *Intermittent*: decelerations that occur with <50% of uterine contractions within a 20-minute period.

-Macones et al. (2008)

73

_____

_____

_____

_____

Early FHR Deceleration

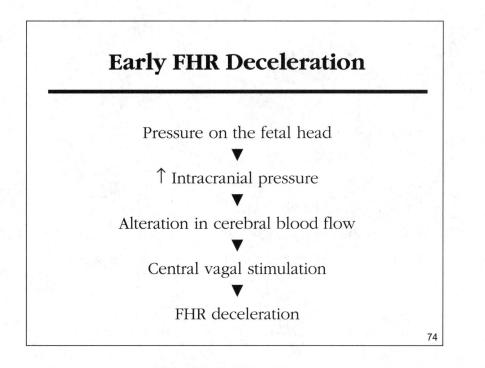

Pressure on the fetal head
▼
↑ Intracranial pressure
▼
Alteration in cerebral blood flow
▼
Central vagal stimulation
▼
FHR deceleration

74

_____

_____

_____

_____

Early FHR Decelerations

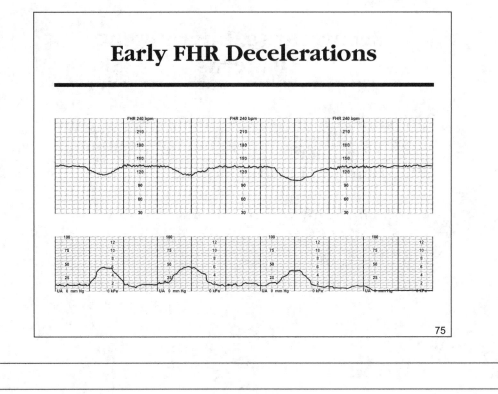

75

Variable Deceleration

Mechanism of Variable Deceleration

PO = Partial Obstruction

CO = Complete Obstruction

UV = Umbilical Vein

UA = Umbilical Artery

FSBP = Fetal Systemic Blood
        Pressure

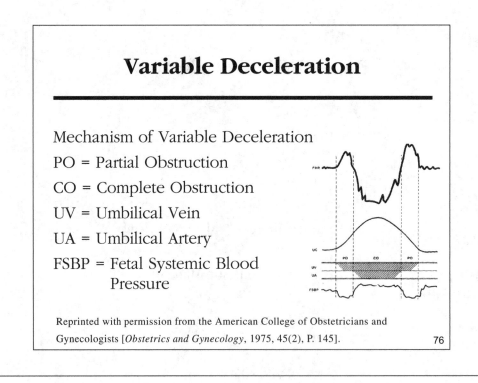

Reprinted with permission from the American College of Obstetricians and
Gynecologists [*Obstetrics and Gynecology*, 1975, 45(2), P. 145].

76

Variable Deceleration

Research is being challenged

Mechanism of Variable Deceleration

PO = Partial Obstruction

CO = Complete Obstruction

UV = Umbilical Vein

UA = Umbilical Artery

FSBP = Fetal Systemic Blood
          Pressure

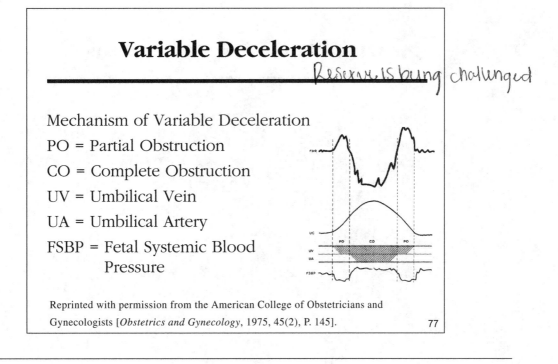

Reprinted with permission from the American College of Obstetricians and Gynecologists [*Obstetrics and Gynecology*, 1975, 45(2), P. 145].

77

Variable FHR Decelerations

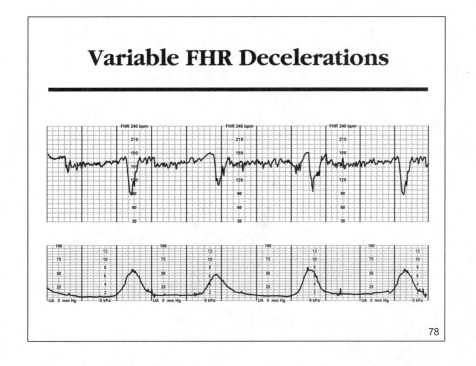

78

Variable FHR Decelerations

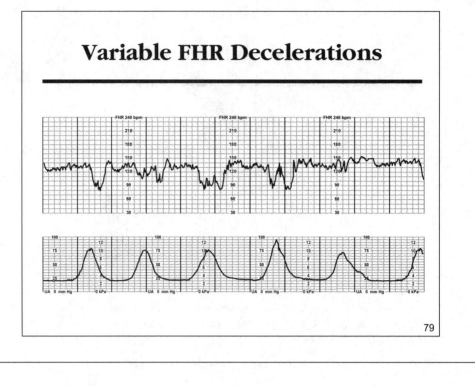

79

Late FHR Decelerations

"Gradual (onset to nadir ≥ 30 seconds) decrease of FHR from baseline and return to baseline associated with uterine contraction

Nadir of deceleration occurs after the peak of the contraction"

-Macones et al. (2008)

80

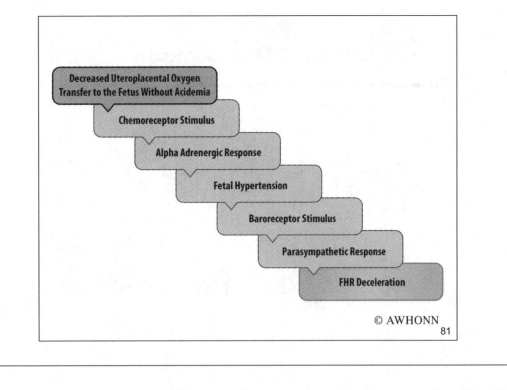

81

_____

_____

_____

_____

Mechanism of Late Decelerations

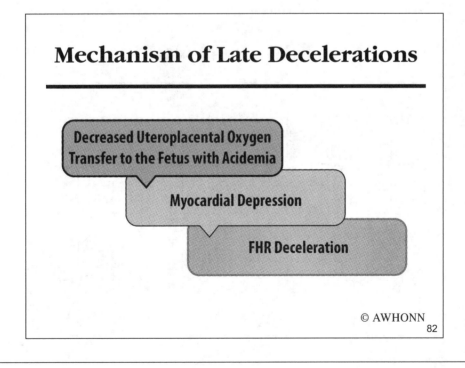

82

_____

_____

_____

_____

Late FHR Decelerations

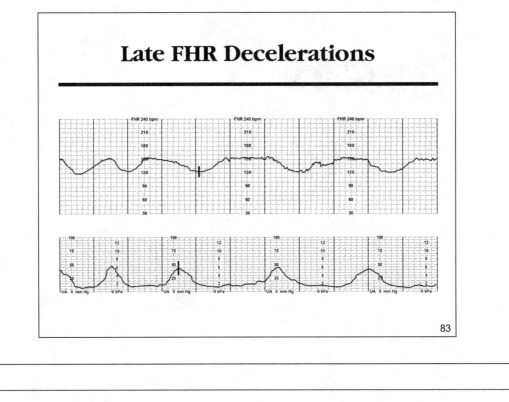

83

Late FHR Decelerations

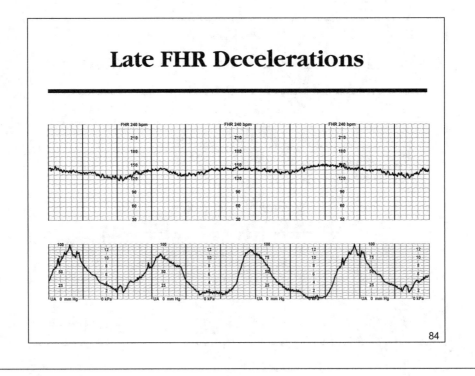

84

Late Decelerations Absent Variability

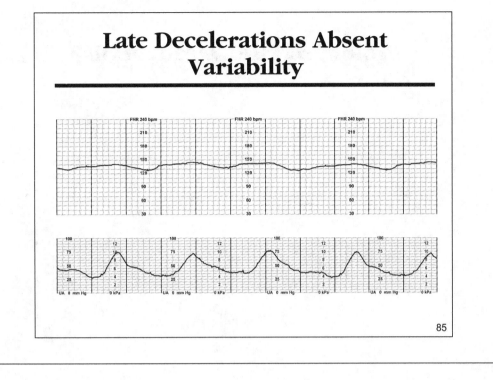

85

Prolonged FHR Decelerations

FHR deceleration of ≥15 bpm from baseline

FHR deceleration lasting ≥2 minutes but <10 minutes

–Macones et al. (2008)

86

Prolonged FHR Deceleration

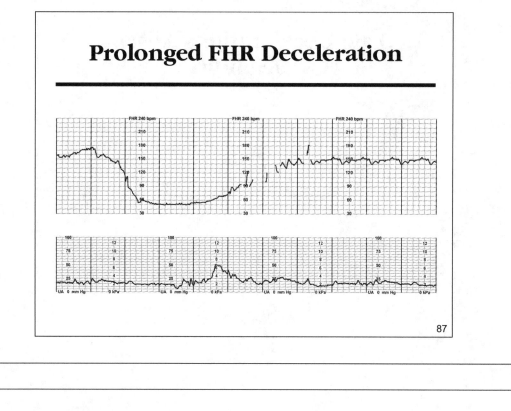

87

Prolonged Decelerations

- Interruption of:
  - Uteroplacental perfusion
  - Umbilical blood flow
- Vagal stimulation

88

Interpretation of FHR Patterns

Three tier FHR interpretation system

- Category I–predicts normal acid-base status

- Category II–indeterminate

- Category III–predicts abnormal acid-base status

–Macones et al. (2008)

89

Category I—Normal FHR Tracing

Includes ALL of the following:
- Baseline FHR 110–160 bpm
- Baseline variability moderate
- Accelerations present or absent
- Early decelerations present or absent
- Late or variable decelerations absent
- Predictive of normal fetal acid-base status
- Follow in routine manner

90

Category II–Indeterminate FHR Tracing

Category II includes all tracings not categorized as Category I or Category III

- Are indeterminate
- Not predictive of abnormal fetal acid-base status; not enough evidence to classify as I or III
- Require evaluation, surveillance, re-evaluation
- This does not mean "no action"

91

Category II–Indeterminate

- Will include many tracings encountered in clinical care
- Examples:
  - Bradycardia without absent variability
  - Tachycardia
  - Minimal baseline variability
  - Absence of induced acceleration after fetal stimulation
  - Prolonged decelerations
  - Recurrent late decelerations with moderate variability

92

Category II–Indeterminate

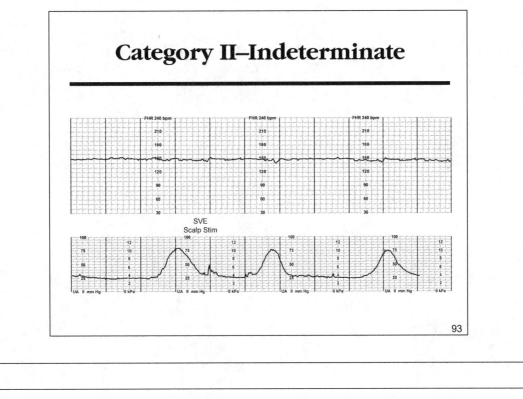

SVE
Scalp Stim

93

Category II–Indeterminate

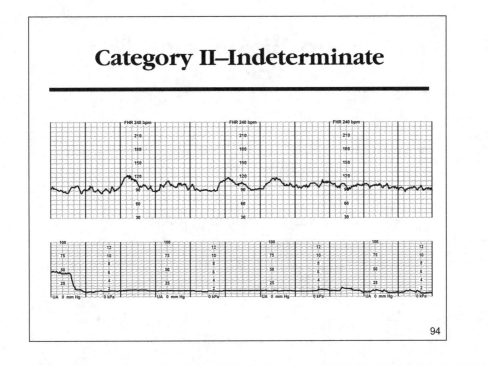

94

Category II–Indeterminate

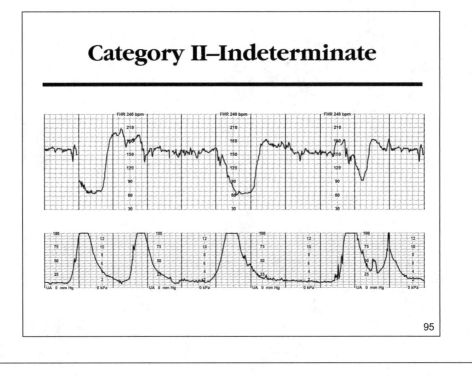

95

Category III–Abnormal FHR Tracings

Include *either*:

- Absent baseline FHR variability and any of the following:
  - ➤ Recurrent late decelerations
  - ➤ Recurrent variable decelerations
  - ➤ Bradycardia OR
  - ➤ Sinusoidal pattern
- Predictive of abnormal fetal acid-base status

96

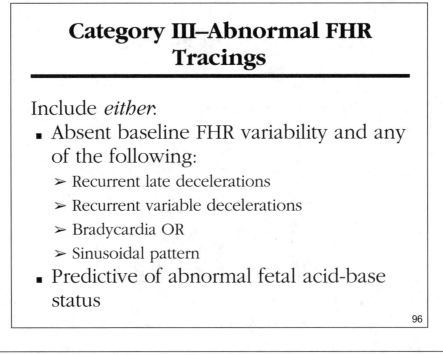

Category III—Abnormal FHR Tracings

- Require prompt evaluation
- Require expeditious resolution

97

Assessing Uterine Activity

- Frequency
- Duration
- Intensity
- Resting tone

98

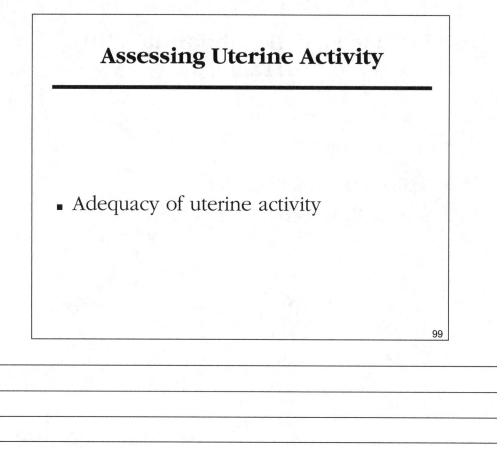

Assessing Uterine Activity

- Adequacy of uterine activity

99

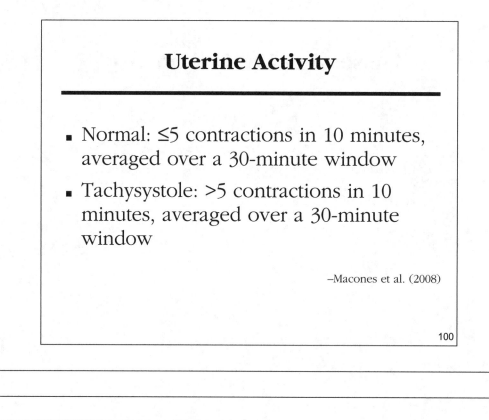

Uterine Activity

- Normal: ≤5 contractions in 10 minutes, averaged over a 30-minute window
- Tachysystole: >5 contractions in 10 minutes, averaged over a 30-minute window

–Macones et al. (2008)

100

Evaluating Uterine Activity

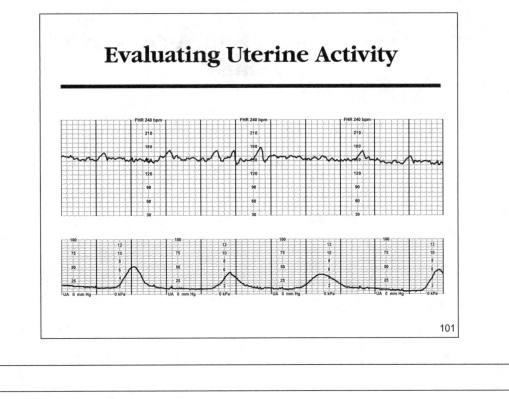

101

Evaluating Uterine Activity

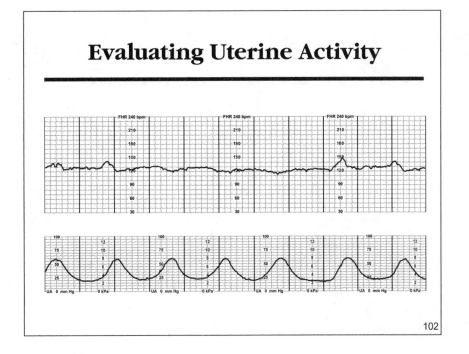

102

Assessment of Fetal Acid-Base Status

- Indirect methods:
  - Fetal scalp stimulation
  - Vibroacoustic stimulation

- Direct methods:
  - Umbilical cord blood sampling

103

Fetal Scalp Stimulation

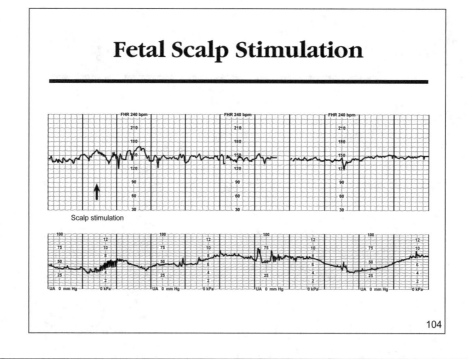

Scalp stimulation

104

NOT for resuscitation

Umbilical Cord Blood Acid-Base Analysis

Respiratory acidosis

- $\uparrow$ CO_2 levels
- Occurs when fetal CO_2 cannot be easily diffused
- Can develop rapidly
- Can be corrected rapidly

Metabolic acidosis

- $\uparrow$ lactic acid levels
- Results from anaerobic metabolism
- Takes longer to develop
- Takes longer to resolve

105

_____

_____

_____

_____

Single Digit Value Guideline

Initial assessment of umbilical cord blood acid-base values

∠7

	Target Values	Metabolic Acidemia	Respiratory Acidemia
pH	≥ 7.10	< 7.10	< 7.10
pO_2 (mm Hg)	> 20	< 20	variable
pCO_2 (mm Hg)	< 60	< 60	> 60
Bicarbonate (mEq/L)	> 22	< 22	≥ 22
BD (mEq/L)	≤ 12	> 12	< 12
BE (mEq/L)	≥ -12	< -12	> -12

Closer to zero is BETTER

106

_____

_____

_____

_____

Types of Acidosis

	pH	pCO$_2$	pO$_2$	BD
Respiratory	▼	▲	Variable	WNL
Metabolic	▼	WNL	▼	▲
Mixed	▼	▲	▼	▲

107

Types of Acidosis

	pH	pCO$_2$	pO$_2$	BD
Respiratory	▼	▲	Variable	WNL
Metabolic	▼	WNL	▼	▲
Mixed	▼	▲	▼	▲

108

Umbilical Arterial Cord Gas Analysis

Case # 1:

- pH   7.22
- pO_2 28
- pCO_2 42
- Bicarbonate   27
- BE   -6

Case # 2:

- pH   6.97
- pO_2 4
- pCO_2 52
- Bicarbonate   2
- BD   18.6

109

Kathleen

- 28 year old G_3P_{2002} at 39 4/7 weeks
- Regular prenatal care
- No prenatal risk factors
- History of two uncomplicated vaginal deliveries
- No abnormal laboratory studies

110

Kathleen: Case Study

- Presents to labor and delivery c/o painful contractions for the last 3 hours
- Membranes intact
- Vital signs: T 98.2°F; BP 128/76; P 84 bpm; RR 18/min.

111

Kathleen: First 30 Minutes Since Admission

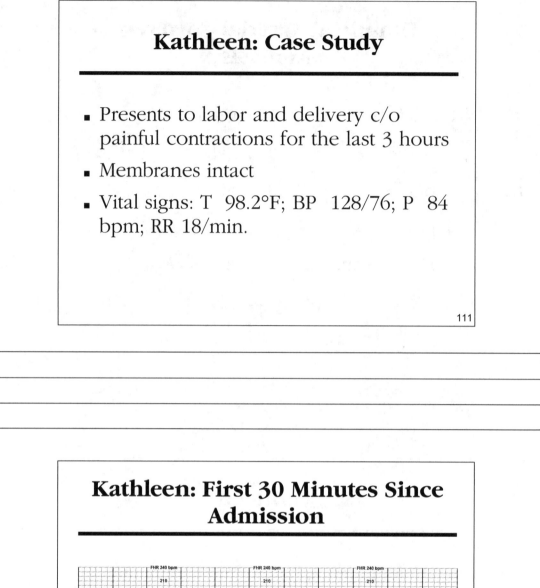

112

Kathleen: First 30 Minutes Since Admission

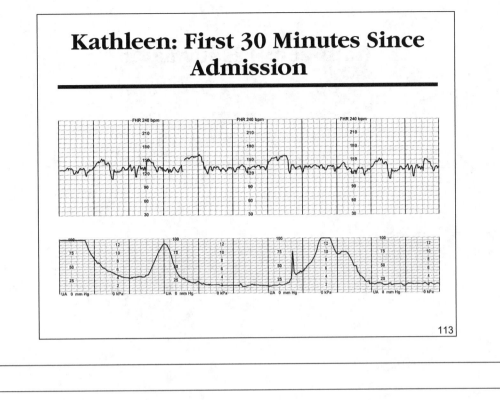

113

Kathleen: 2 Hours Later

Kathleen calls the nurse to the room stating, "I think my water just broke."

- SVE reveals gross rupture of membranes with clear fluid, moderate amount

- 8 cm/100%/0

114

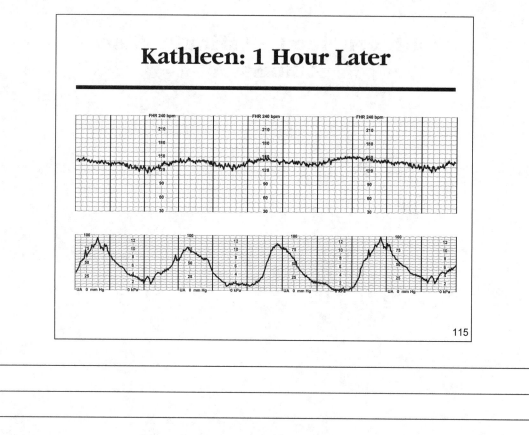

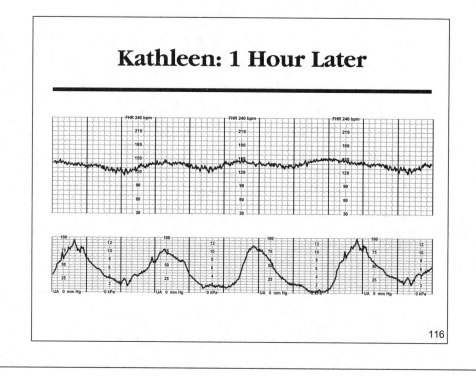

Kathleen: 30 Minutes Later

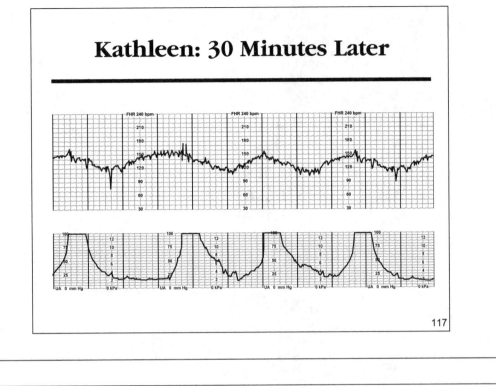

117

Kathleen

- Second stage of labor lasted 22 minutes
- EFM tracing continued to exhibit moderate variability and recurrent late decelerations
- What type of outcome would you anticipate for Kathleen and her baby?

118

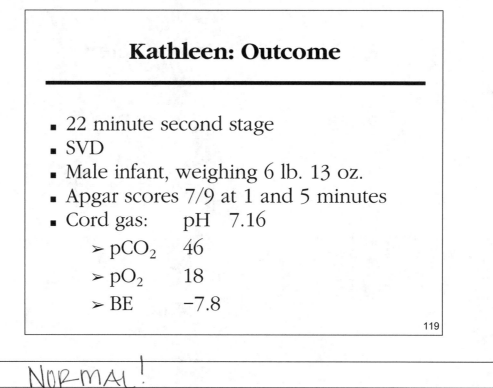

Kathleen: Outcome

- 22 minute second stage
- SVD
- Male infant, weighing 6 lb. 13 oz.
- Apgar scores 7/9 at 1 and 5 minutes
- Cord gas: pH 7.16
    - pCO_2 46
    - pO_2 18
    - BE −7.8

119

NORMAL!

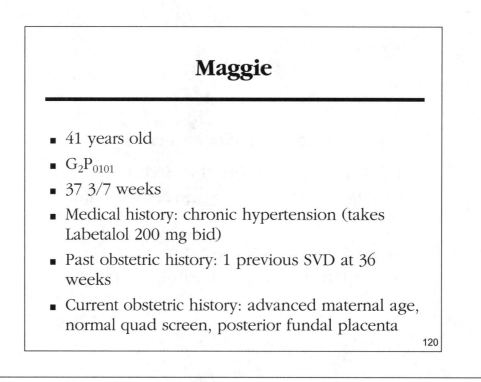

Maggie

- 41 years old
- G_2P_{0101}
- 37 3/7 weeks
- Medical history: chronic hypertension (takes Labetalol 200 mg bid)
- Past obstetric history: 1 previous SVD at 36 weeks
- Current obstetric history: advanced maternal age, normal quad screen, posterior fundal placenta

120

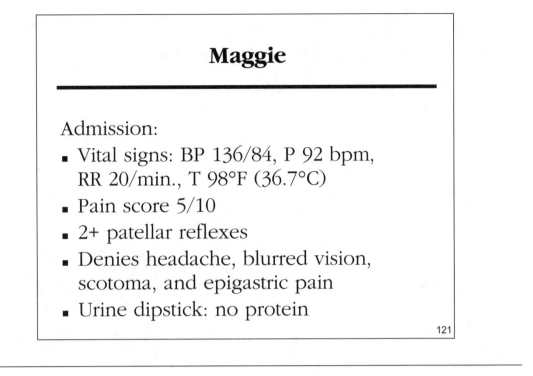

Maggie

Admission:
- Vital signs: BP 136/84, P 92 bpm, RR 20/min., T 98°F (36.7°C)
- Pain score 5/10
- 2+ patellar reflexes
- Denies headache, blurred vision, scotoma, and epigastric pain
- Urine dipstick: no protein

121

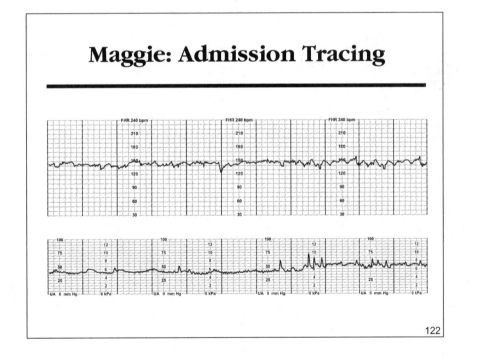

Maggie: Admission Tracing

122

Maggie: 3 Hours Later

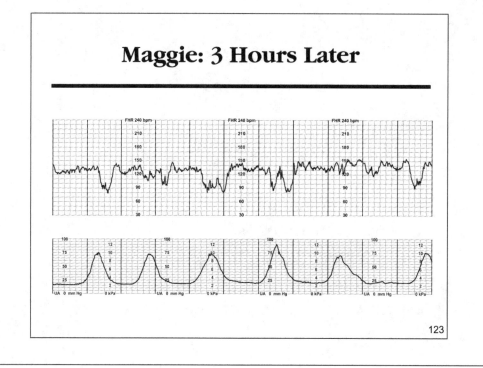

123

Maggie: 1½ Hours Later

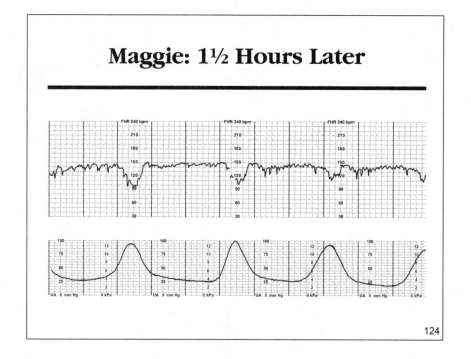

124

Maggie: 1 Hour Later

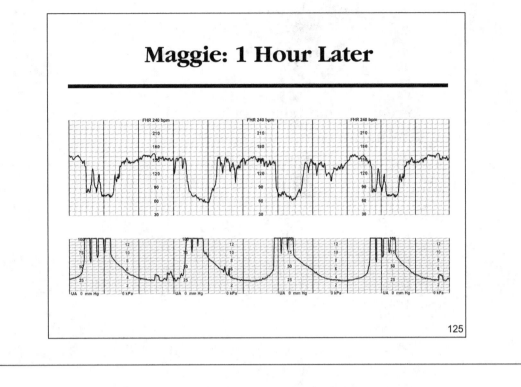

125

Maggie: 20 Minutes Later

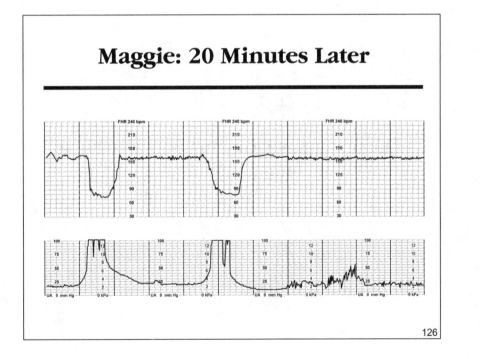

126

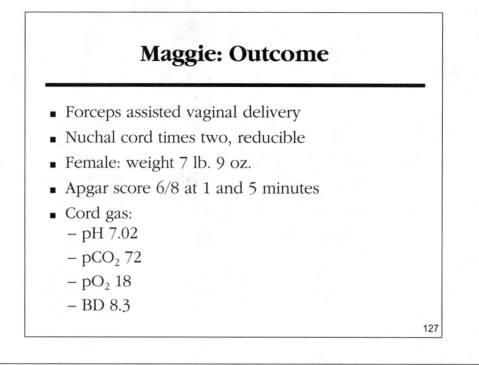

Maggie: Outcome

- Forceps assisted vaginal delivery
- Nuchal cord times two, reducible
- Female: weight 7 lb. 9 oz.
- Apgar score 6/8 at 1 and 5 minutes
- Cord gas:
  - pH 7.02
  - pCO_2 72
  - pO_2 18
  - BD 8.3

127

Respiratory acidosis

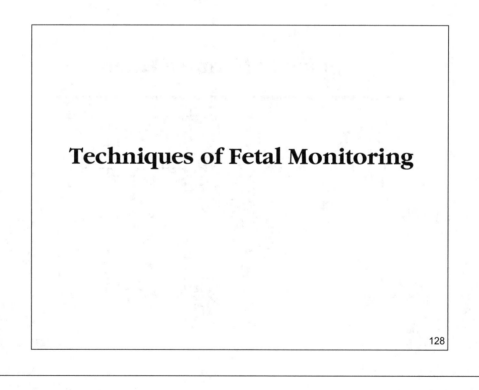

Techniques of Fetal Monitoring

128

FHR and Uterine Activity Monitoring

- Most women in the United States and Canada have continuous EFM during labor

- Knowledge about ALL methods of FHR and UA monitoring is necessary

129

Intermittent Auscultation

- Intermittent counting of the FHR—fetoscope or hand-held Doppler ultrasound:
  - ➤ Fetoscope detects heart sounds
  - ➤ Doppler detects reflected sound from heart motion

- Fetoscope can be used for troubleshooting:
  - ➤ Verification of FHR arrhythmias
  - ➤ Clarification of maternal heart rate vs. fetal heart rate, or halving or doubling of the FHR on the EFM tracing

130

Capabilities of Auscultation Devices

The fetoscope:
- Detects FHR baseline
- Detects FHR rhythm
- Verifies presence of irregular rhythm
- Detects increases (accelerations) and decreases (decelerations) from FHR baseline
- Clarifies double counting or half-counting by EFM

The Doppler:
- Detects FHR baseline
- Detects FHR rhythm
- Detects increases (accelerations) and decreases (decelerations)

–Feinstein, Sprague, and Trepanier (2008)

131

Auscultation Techniques and Procedure

- Palpate abdomen for fetal position
- Place fetoscope bell or the Doppler transducer over fetal back
- Verify FHR by assessing maternal pulse
- Determine FHR baseline
  - ➢ Count for 30–60 seconds between contractions initially
  - ➢ Count for 15–60 seconds between contractions at prescribed intervals

132

Interpreting Auscultation Findings

Category I FHR characteristics by auscultation include all of the following:

- Normal FHR baseline between 110 and 160 bpm
- Regular rhythm
- Presence of or absence of FHR increases or accelerations from the baseline rate
- Absence of FHR decreases or decelerations from the baseline

133

Interpreting Auscultation Findings

Category II FHR characteristics by auscultation include any of the following:

- Irregular rhythm
- Presence of FHR decreases or decelerations from the baseline
- Tachycardia (baseline >160 bpm > 10 minutes in duration)
- Bradycardia (baseline <110 bpm > 10 minutes in duration)

134

Benefits of Auscultation

- Increased hands-on time with patient
- Neonatal outcomes compare favorably with EFM based on limited RCTs for low-risk patients
- Lower cesarean birth rates
- Freedom of maternal movement and increased ambulation

135

Limitations of Auscultation

- FHR assessment may be limited by fetal/ maternal position/movement, maternal size or uterine tension
- 1:1 nurse/patient ratio may require staffing realignment
- Requires education, practice, skill

136

Limitations of Auscultation

- Auscultation is not continuous
- FHR variability and identification of decelerations cannot be assessed
- No tracing generated for collaborative decision making and record keeping

137

Frequency of Intermittent Auscultation

	Latent phase (<4 cm)	Latent phase (4–5 cm)	Active phase (>6 cm)	Second stage (passive fetal descent)	Second stage (active pushing)
Low-risk without oxytocin	At least hourly	Every 15–30 minutes	Every 15–30 minutes	Every 15 minutes	Every 5–15 minutes

138

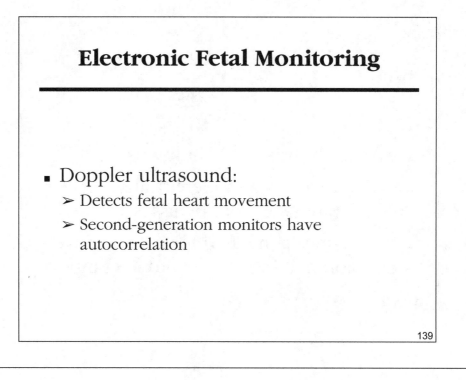

Electronic Fetal Monitoring

- Doppler ultrasound:
  - ➤ Detects fetal heart movement
  - ➤ Second-generation monitors have autocorrelation

139

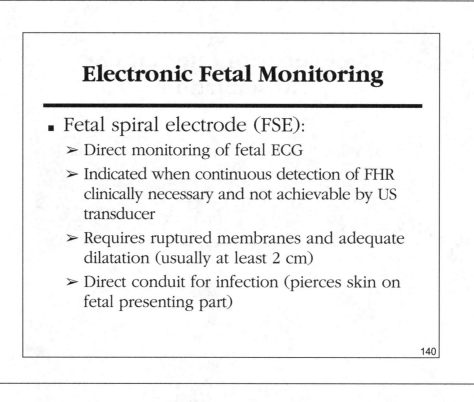

Electronic Fetal Monitoring

- Fetal spiral electrode (FSE):
  - ➤ Direct monitoring of fetal ECG
  - ➤ Indicated when continuous detection of FHR clinically necessary and not achievable by US transducer
  - ➤ Requires ruptured membranes and adequate dilatation (usually at least 2 cm)
  - ➤ Direct conduit for infection (pierces skin on fetal presenting part)

140

Electronic Fetal Monitoring

- Benefits of Doppler Ultrasound:
  - ➤ Non-invasive
  - ➤ May be intermittent or continuous
  - ➤ Provides a permanent record
  - ➤ Records baseline rate, variability, and FHR patterns
- Limitations of Doppler Ultrasound:
  - ➤ May restrict maternal movement
  - ➤ Signal transmission may be affected by maternal position or size as well as fetal position or movement
- May still build in slight differences in variability

141

Troubleshooting and Corrective Measures

- Confirm fetal position
- Adjust monitor belt
- Reapply monitor gel
- Reposition ultrasound transducer and/or reposition the mother
- Use real-time ultrasound
- Application of FSE

142

Troubleshooting

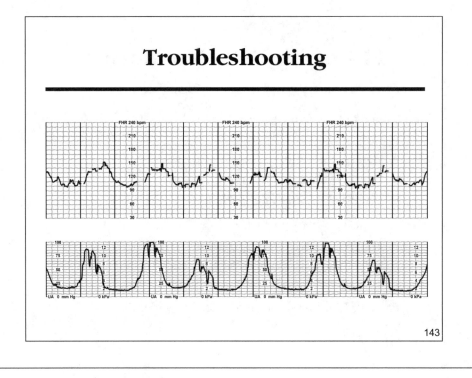

143

Indeterminant baseline

Electronic Fetal Monitoring

Doppler Ultrasound
- Signal ambiguity
  - The fetal signal is replaced by an alternate signal from the mother or another fetus

144

Troubleshooting

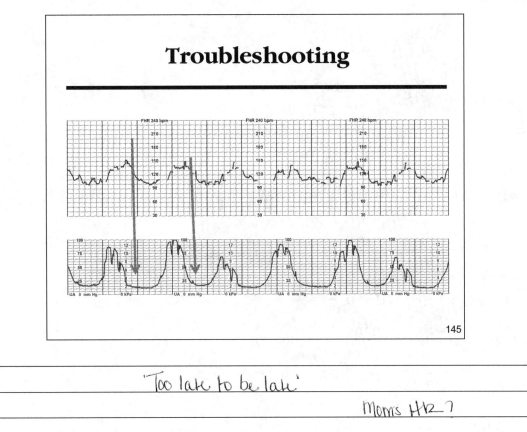

145

'Too late to be late'

Mom's HR ?

Electronic Fetal Monitoring

Doppler Ultrasound

– Artifact:

➤ Results from mechanical limitations of the monitor, electronic interference or weak signal

➤ Appears as gaps or dots with external monitoring and as irregular lines of varying lengths with an FSE

146

Artifact

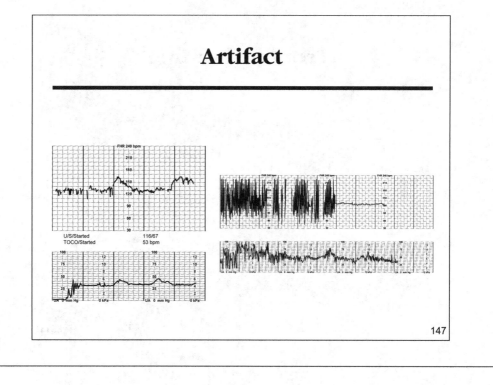

147

Electronic Fetal Monitoring

- Benefits of fetal spiral electrode (FSE):
  - ➤ Provides continuous tracing of FHR
  - ➤ Maternal position change does not affect quality of FHR tracing

- Limitations of FSE:
  - ➤ Invasive
  - ➤ Requires ROM and adequate cervical dilation
  - ➤ Contraindicated with placenta previa and certain infections
  - ➤ Potential risk of infection
  - ➤ Electronic interference and artifact may occur

148

Troubleshooting the FSE and Corrective Actions

- Confirm FHR by ausculation
- Check connections to monitor, electrode, and cable
- Turn off the logic switch
- Check FSE placement and reapply if necessary
- Confirm maternal pulse simultaneously with FHR

149

Recommendations for Assessment of Fetal Status during Labor
When Using Electronic Fetal Monitoring[a,b]

	Latent phase (<4 cm)	Latent phase (4–5 cm)	Active phase (>6 cm)	Second stage (passive fetal descent)	Second stage (active pushing)
Low-risk without oxytocin	At least hourly	Every 30 minutes	Every 30 minutes	Every 15 minutes	Every 15 minutes
With oxytocin or risk factors	Every 15 minutes with oxytocin; every 30 minutes without	Every 15 minutes	Every 15 minutes	Every 15 minutes	Every 5 minutes

150

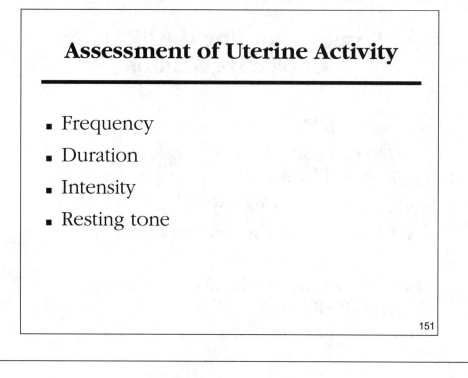

Assessment of Uterine Activity

- Frequency
- Duration
- Intensity
- Resting tone

151

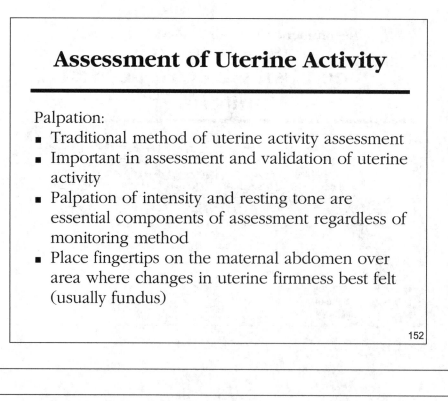

Assessment of Uterine Activity

Palpation:
- Traditional method of uterine activity assessment
- Important in assessment and validation of uterine activity
- Palpation of intensity and resting tone are essential components of assessment regardless of monitoring method
- Place fingertips on the maternal abdomen over area where changes in uterine firmness best felt (usually fundus)

152

Assessment of Uterine Activity

Tocodynamometer transducer (Toco):
- Detects changes in shape of abdomen resulting from uterine tension
- Place pressure sensor on abdomen over uterine fundus at point of maximum contraction intensity
- Tracing is accurate for frequency and duration only
- Use in conjunction with palpation

153

Assessment of Uterine Activity

- Intrauterine pressure catheter (IUPC):
  - ➤ Quantitative measurement for strength of contractions and resting tone
- Three types:
  - ➤ Transducer tipped
  - ➤ Sensor tipped
  - ➤ Fluid filled
- Not always indicated during labor

154

Benefits of IUPC's

- Accurate assessment of frequency, duration, and intensity of uterine contractions and resting tone
- Withdrawal of amniotic fluid for testing
- Amnioinfusion port
- May be recalibrated or flushed to validate accuracy of internal monitoring

155

Troubleshooting the IUPC

- Verify IUPC position (check markings at perineum and have patient cough)
- Flush catheter if needed
- Recalibrate if:
  - ➤ Resting tone too high/too low despite palpation of soft uterus
  - ➤ No contractions noted but able to palpate contractions
  - ➤ Artifact present
- Check monitor for loose connections or re-zero IUPC as needed
- Run monitor's self-test feature

156

Calculating Montevideo Units (MVUs)

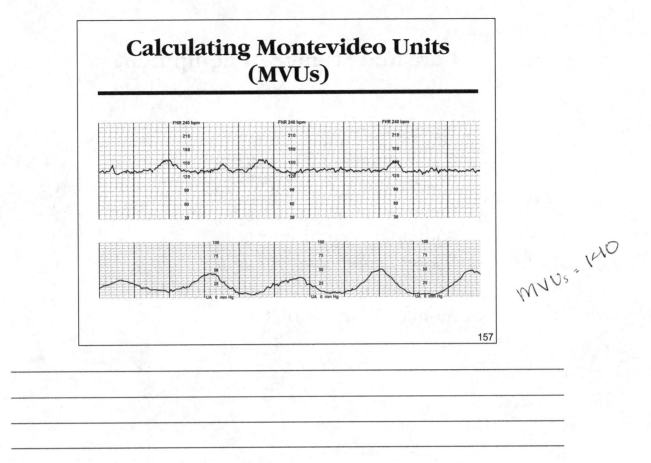

MVUs = 140

157

_____

_____

_____

_____

Comparison of Uterine Contraction Assessment

- Patient perception
  - ➢ Maybe not until 15–30 mmHg
- Manual palpation
  - ➢ 10–15 mmHg
- Internal monitor
  - ➢ 10 mmHg

158

_____

_____

_____

_____

Care and Storage of Equipment

- Handle carefully
- Never immerse transducers or cables in water, unless indicated by manufacturer
- Clean monitor, transducers, and cables with approved disinfectant
- Loosely coil cables for storage
- Don't force insertion of cables into monitors if they don't fit

159

Techniques Summary

- Methods for assessing FHR
- Methods for assessing uterine contractions
- Benefits and limitations of each method
- Troubleshooting monitor information
- Clinical decisions regarding choice of monitoring method
- Patient and professional education are imperative

160

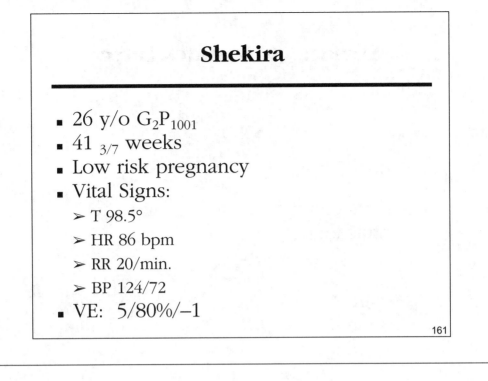

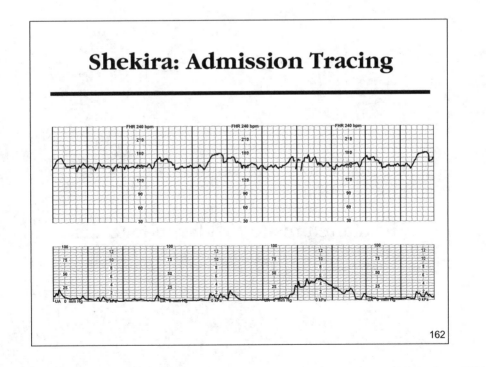

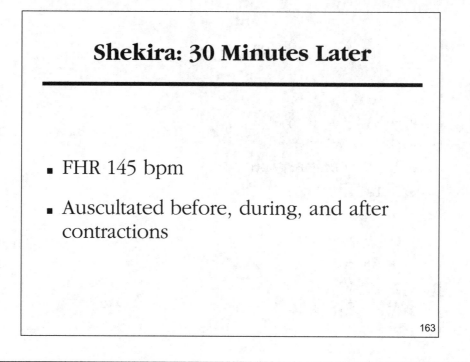

Shekira: 30 Minutes Later

- FHR 145 bpm

- Auscultated before, during, and after contractions

163

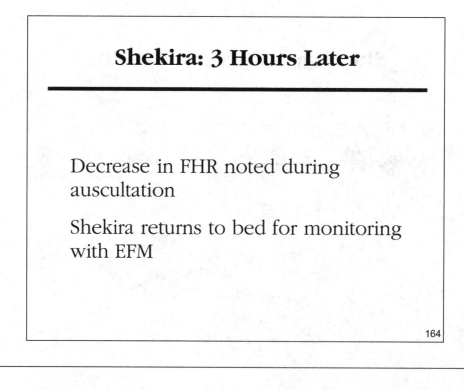

Shekira: 3 Hours Later

Decrease in FHR noted during auscultation

Shekira returns to bed for monitoring with EFM

164

Shekira: EFM

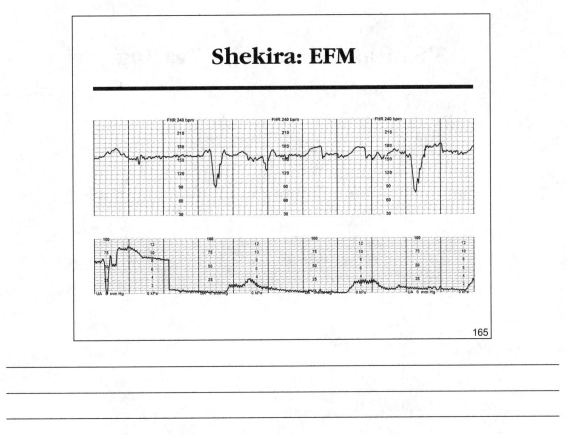

165

Shekira: 1 Hour Later

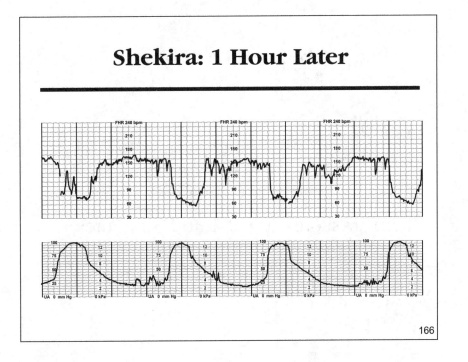

166

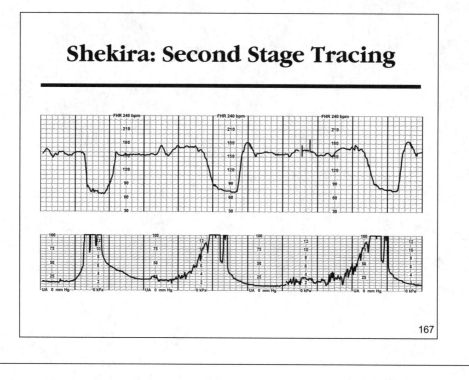

Shekira: Second Stage Tracing

167

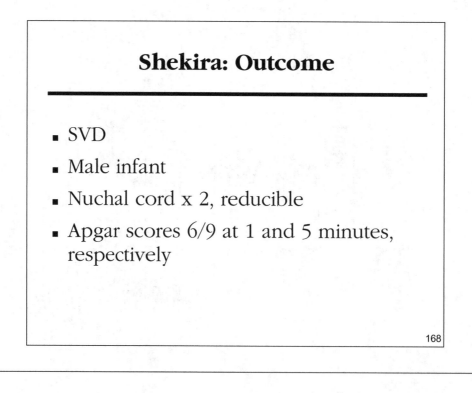

Shekira: Outcome

- SVD
- Male infant
- Nuchal cord x 2, reducible
- Apgar scores 6/9 at 1 and 5 minutes, respectively

168

Annie

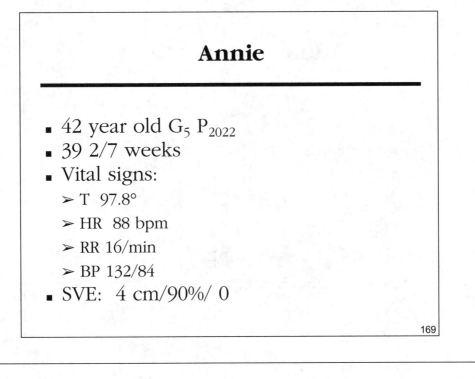

- 42 year old G_5 P_{2022}
- 39 2/7 weeks
- Vital signs:
  - T 97.8°
  - HR 88 bpm
  - RR 16/min
  - BP 132/84
- SVE: 4 cm/90%/ 0

169

Annie: Tracing

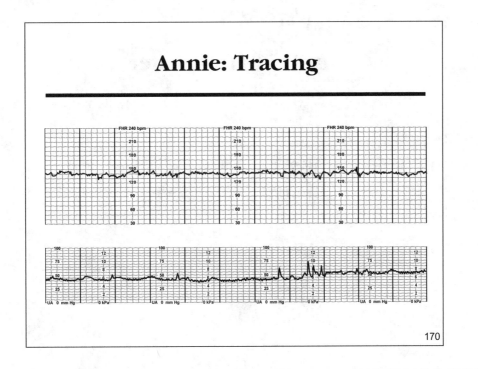

170

Annie: 2 Hours Later

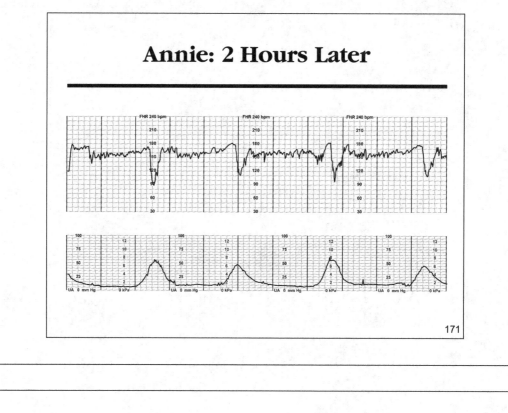

171

Annie: 1 Hour Later

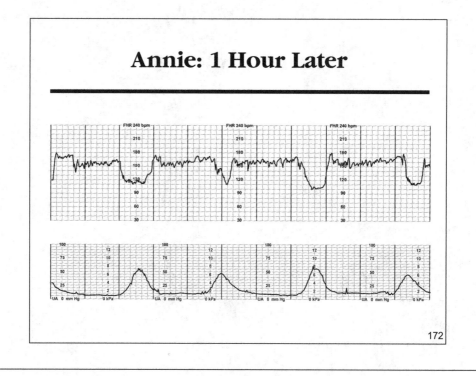

172

Annie: 30 Minutes Later

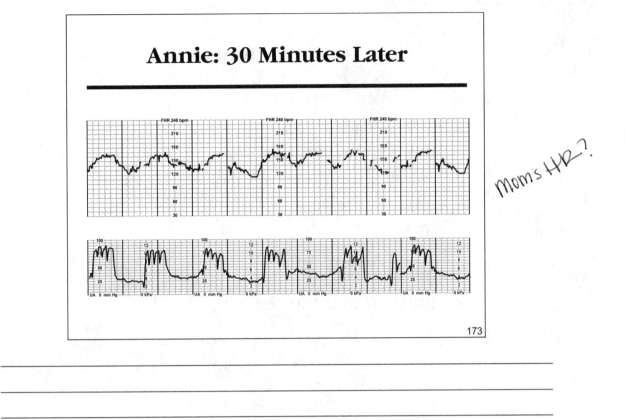

Mom's HR?

173

Annie: 20 Minutes Later

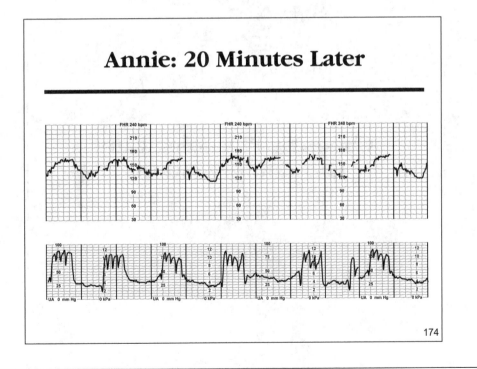

174

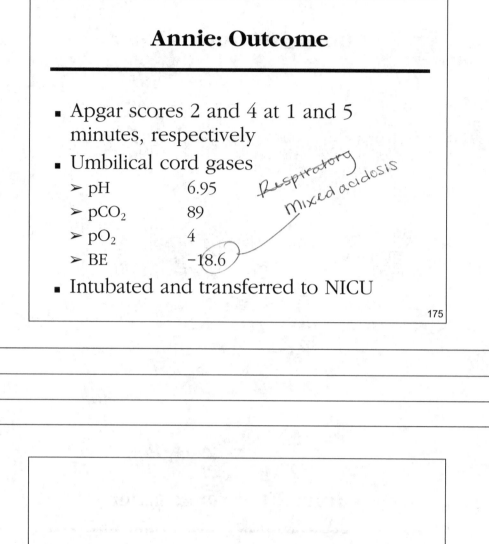

Annie: Outcome

- Apgar scores 2 and 4 at 1 and 5 minutes, respectively
- Umbilical cord gases
  - ➢ pH   6.95
  - ➢ pCO_2 89
  - ➢ pO_2 4
  - ➢ BE   −18.6
- Intubated and transferred to NICU

Respiratory Mixed acidosis

175

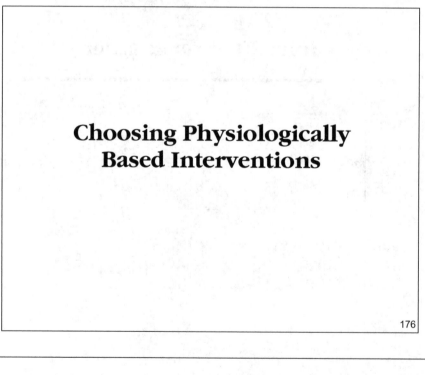

Choosing Physiologically Based Interventions

176

Physiologic Goals

- Support maternal coping and labor progress
- Maximize uterine blood flow
- Maximize umbilical circulation
- Maximize oxygenation
- Maintain appropriate uterine activity

177

Maternal Catecholamine Release

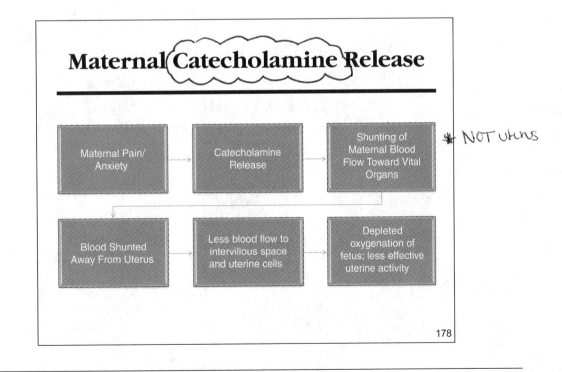

\# NOT uterus

178

Support Coping and Labor Progress

- Review plans/expectations with the woman and her partner, friends, or family

- Maintain calm environment whenever possible

- Include family members where appropriate

179

Support Coping and Labor Progress and Judicious Use of Technology

- Presence at the bedside

- Selection of monitoring methods based on needs

180

Support Coping and Labor Progress and Judicious Use of Technology

- Use of frequent position changes/ upright positioning

- Minimize technology and avoid unnecessary interventions when possible

181

Determining Interventions and Goals

- Cervical exam

- Review of uterine activity and palpation of tone

- Evaluation of maternal vital signs

- Assessment of unit resources

182

Maximize Uterine Blood Flow

- Reduce anxiety/pain
- Maternal position
  - ➤ Lateral positioning
- Hydration
- Medication to reduce uterine activity

183

Maternal Position

Position	Mean Cardiac Output (liters per minute)
Left lateral	6.6
Right lateral	6.8
Supine	6.0
Sitting	6.2
Standing	5.4
Knee Chest	6.9

Clark, et. al. 1991

184

Maternal Position

Fetal oxygen saturation was higher when the maternal position was left or right lateral than when in the supine position

-Simpson and James (2005)

185

Hydration

Effect on the course of labor:

– Increased IVF (250 mL/hour vs. 125 mL/hour)—lower frequency of prolonged labor and possibly less need for oxytocin

-Garite, Weeks, Peters-Phan, Pattillo, and Brewster (2000)

– IVF vs. oral hydration—those receiving IVF had shorter labor duration

-Direkvand-Maghadam and Rezaeian (2012)

– Increased IVF (250 mL/hour vs. 125 mL/hour) in active labor associated with shorter labor duration and lower frequency of both prolonged labor and oxytocin use

- Eslamian, Marsoosi, and Pakneeyat (2006)

186

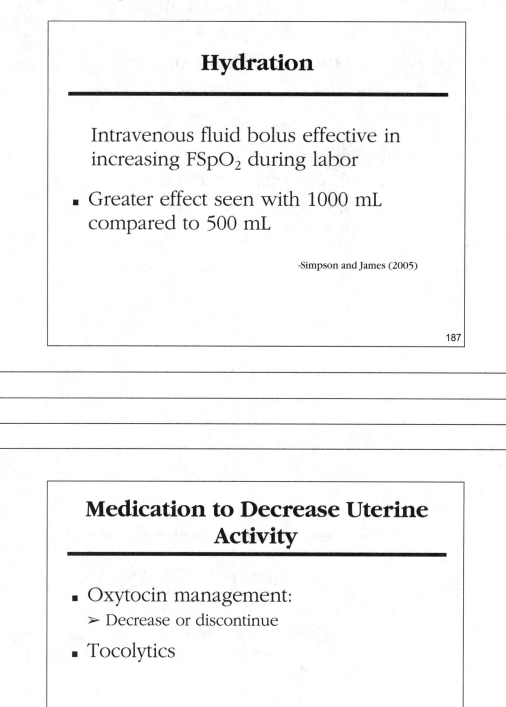

Hydration

Intravenous fluid bolus effective in increasing FSpO$_2$ during labor

- Greater effect seen with 1000 mL compared to 500 mL

-Simpson and James (2005)

187

Medication to Decrease Uterine Activity

- Oxytocin management:
  - ➤ Decrease or discontinue
- Tocolytics

188

Maximize Umbilical Circulation

- Maternal positioning
- Amnioinfusion:
  - ➤ Protocols vary
  - ➤ Continuous and intermittent infusions similarly effective
  - ➤ Continuous EFM recommended to determine if variable decelerations resolve
  - ➤ Closely monitor resting tone for need to discontinue infusion

189

Maximize Oxygenation
Placental and Umbilical Blood Vessel Gas

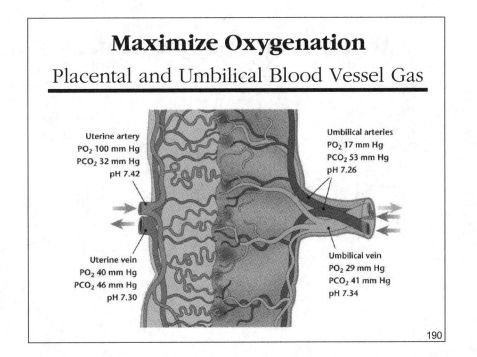

Uterine artery
PO$_2$ 100 mm Hg
PCO$_2$ 32 mm Hg
pH 7.42

Umbilical arteries
PO$_2$ 17 mm Hg
PCO$_2$ 53 mm Hg
pH 7.26

Uterine vein
PO$_2$ 40 mm Hg
PCO$_2$ 46 mm Hg
pH 7.30

Umbilical vein
PO$_2$ 29 mm Hg
PCO$_2$ 41 mm Hg
pH 7.34

190

Administering Supplemental Oxygen

- Increases maternal blood oxygen tension

- Increases fetal oxygen saturation

191

Administering Supplemental Oxygen

- Given at 10 L per minute via nonrebreather mask

192

Potential Adverse Effects of Supplemental Oxygen

- Potential for creation of oxygen free radicals
- Little data available on effect of long-term administration
- Use other resuscitative techniques first
- Remove other sources of stress
- Discontinue as soon as possible

193

_____

_____

_____

_____

Maximize Oxygenation

- Maternal breathing
- Supplemental oxygen:
  - ➤ Cautious use
  - ➤ Not first line or sole measure
  - ➤ Not for prophylactic administration

194

_____

_____

_____

_____

Maintain Appropriate Uterine Activity

- Tachysystole:
  - > 5 contractions in 10 minutes averaged over 30 minutes
- Normal uterine activity:
  - ≤5 contractions in 10 minutes averaged over 30 minutes

–Macones, et. al., 2008

195

_____

_____

_____

_____

Assessing Contractions

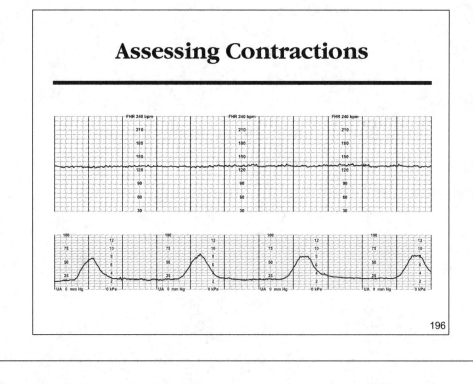

196

_____

_____

_____

_____

Assessing Contractions

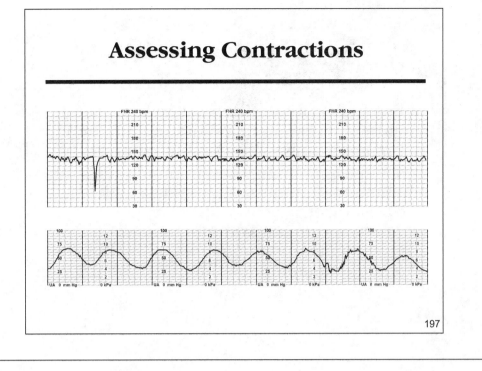

197

Calculating Normal Uterine Activity

- Internal uterine pressure catheter (IUPC)
- Montevideo units: subtract resting tone from peak uterine activity for each contraction in a 10-minute period
- Caldeyro-Barcia and Poseiro study:
  - ➤ Labor began clinically when MVUs rose to 80–120 with contraction strength of >40 mmHg; equates to 2–3 contractions with >40 mm Hg intensity every 10 min
  - ➤ First stage: 100–250 MVUs, frequency 3–5 every 10 min
  - ➤ Second stage: 300–400 MVUs, frequency 5–6 every 10 min

198

Normal Uterine Activity

- Uterine contractions that palpate as moderate or stronger are likely to have peaks of ≥50 mm Hg
- First stage of labor: contraction intensity 40–70 mm Hg
- Second stage of labor: contraction intensity 80 mm Hg or more
- Relaxation time: ≥60 seconds in first stage

  ≥45 seconds in second stage

199

Inter-Contraction Interval

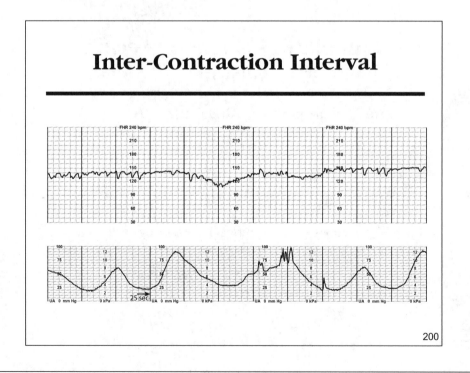

200

Assessing Contraction Intervals

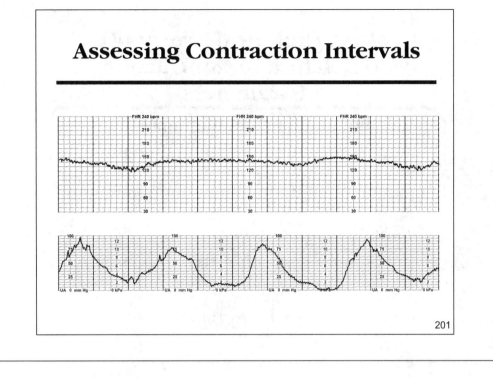

201

Relaxation Time

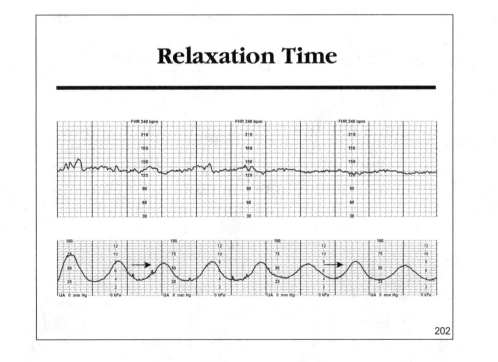

202

Mean Umbilical Artery pH in Relation to Contraction Parameters

Last hour of first stage of labor:

Average relaxation time (seconds):

pH ≤ 7.11 (51)

pH ≥ 7.12 (63)

Second stage of labor:

Average relaxation time (seconds):

pH ≤ 7.11 (36)

pH ≥ 7.12 (47)

203

Fetal Oxygen Saturation

- Initial rise at beginning of a contraction

- Oxygen saturation declines after initial increase and persists until the contraction has ended

- Ideal contraction interval in which fetal cerebral oxygen saturation remains stable or increases is 2.3 minutes or longer

204

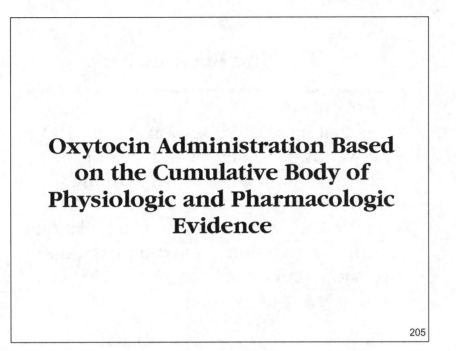

Oxytocin Administration Based on the Cumulative Body of Physiologic and Pharmacologic Evidence

205

Pharmacokinetics of Oxytocin

- Half-life 10–12 minutes
- 3–4 half-lives are needed to reach steady-state plasma concentration
- Full effect of oxytocin cannot be evaluated until steady-state concentration is achieved
- The basis for recommendations for 30–40 minute interval dosing of oxytocin

206

Uterine Response

- Gradual increase in response from 20 to 30 weeks, followed by a plateau from 34 weeks until term, when sensitivity increases
- Lower BMI and greater cervical dilation, parity or gestational age are predictors of successful response to oxytocin for induction

207

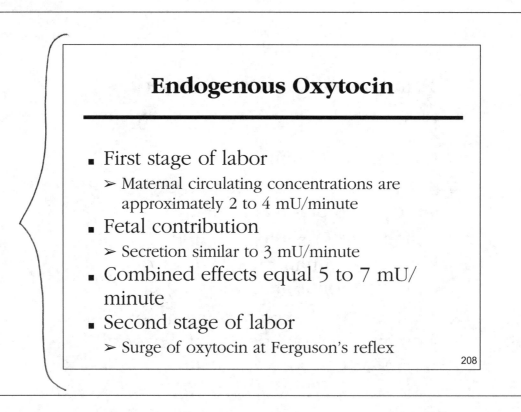

Endogenous Oxytocin

- First stage of labor
  - ➤ Maternal circulating concentrations are approximately 2 to 4 mU/minute
- Fetal contribution
  - ➤ Secretion similar to 3 mU/minute
- Combined effects equal 5 to 7 mU/ minute
- Second stage of labor
  - ➤ Surge of oxytocin at Ferguson's reflex

208

Oxytocin Dosage

- Low-dose regimen:
  - ➤ Starting dose of 0.5–2 mU/minute
  - ➤ Increase 1–2 mU/minute every 30–60 minutes
  - ➤ Use lowest possible dose to achieve physiologic affect

- There is no data that more oxytocin will improve dysfunctional labor

209

Adequate Labor

- Uterine contractions that produce cervical change

- "Adequate labor" may be achieved by:
  - ➤ Contractions every 2–3 minutes, lasting 80–90 seconds and palpating strong or
  - ➤ Consistent achievement of 200–220 MVUs

210

Oxytocin Dosage

Based on the evidence:
- Continuing oxytocin after active labor is established will not shorten labor
- Long duration and high dose may have opposite intended effect on course of labor by desensitizing uterine receptors to exogenous and endogenous oxytocin
- Labor is generally self-sustaining once active phase is established

211

Oxytocin-Induced Tachystole

Oxytocin-Induced Tachysystole (Normal FHR)
Assist patient to lateral position
Intravenous fluid bolus of at least 500 ml LR as indicated
If uterine activity does not return to normal after 10–15 min, ▼ oxytocin rate by at least ½. If uterine activity does not return to normal after additional 10–15 min, discontinue oxytocin.
After resolution of tachysystole-if infusion off <20–30 min, resume oxytocin at no more than ½ rate that was infusion at time of tachysystole. If infusion off >30–40 min, resume oxytocin at initial dose of administration.

- Simpson and O'Brien-Abel (2013)

212

Oxytocin-Induced Tachysystole

Oxytocin Induced Tachysystole Protocol (Abnormal FHR)
Discontinue oxytocin
Assist patient to lateral position
Administer intravenous fluid bolus of at least 500 mL LR as indicated
Consider oxygen at 10 L/minute via non-rebreather mask; discontinue as soon as possible based on FHR pattern.
If no response, consider .25 mg terbutaline subcutaneous
To resume after resolution of tachystole; if infusion off for <20–30 minute, resume at no more than ½ rate that was infusing when tachysystole occurred. If infusion off for > 30–40 minute, resume oxytocin at initial dose of administration.

- Simpson and O'Brien-Abel (2013)

213

Oxytocin is High-Alert Medication

- Institute for Safe Medication Practices designated IV oxytocin as a high-alert medication in 2007

- Medication errors involving IV oxytocin are dose-related and commonly involve excessive uterine activity with subsequent fetal response

214

Strategies for Minimizing Risk of Harm

Standardized process for oxytocin administration:

- Elective labor induction only after 39 weeks of gestation
- Standard protocols/order sets based on current physiologic and pharmacologic evidence
- Standard concentration of oxytocin prepared by pharmacy

-Simpson (2008) and Simpson and Knox (2009)   215

Strategies for Minimizing Risk of Harm

- Standard definition of the desired effect of the oxytocin administration
- Standard definition of uterine tachysystole
- Standard treatment of oxytocin-induced uterine tachysystole guided by fetal status
- Communication with provider when oxytocin is discontinued due to tachysystole or abnormal FHR tracing characteristics

216

Strategies for Minimizing Risk of Harm

Methods to mitigate harm that may result from error:

- Protocols that allow discontinuing or decreasing the dose without contacting the physician or nurse midwife
- Availability of consensus rescue protocols

-Simpson (2008) and Simpson and Knox (2009)

217

Second Stage Labor

- Increased contraction frequency and strength are common
- Indeterminate or abnormal FHR patterns may occur
- Increase in frequency of late, variable, or prolonged decelerations or a decrease in FHR variability is associated with lower Apgar scores and higher incidence of metabolic acidosis

218

Second Stage Labor Care

Second Stage Labor Care to Promote Fetal Well-Being
If no urge to push, consider delaying pushing for up to 2 hours for nulliparous and up to 1 hour for multiparous
Discourage prolonged breath-holding
Discourage more than 3 pushing efforts per contraction and more than 6–8 seconds of each pushing effort
Close observation of FHR. Consider pushing every other or every 3rd contraction to avoid recurrent FHR decelerations
Avoid tachysystole

-AWHONN (2008)

219

Emily's Case Study

- Emily is a 16 y/o G_1 P_0 @ 41 $_{3/7}$ weeks

- No significant past medical history

- Late entry into prenatal care (8 total visits)

- Normal prenatal labs

220

Emily: Admission Tracing 0700

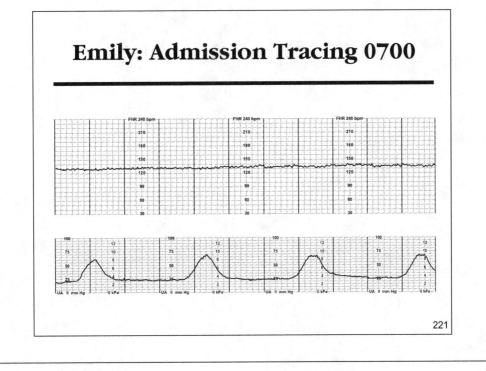

221

Emily: Admission Assessment

- SVE: 2 cm/80%/–2 /anterior with a medium consistency

- Cephalic presentation noted

- Vital signs: BP 124/72; HR 86 bpm; RR 20/min.; T 97.4° F

222

Emily: 2 Hours Later 0900

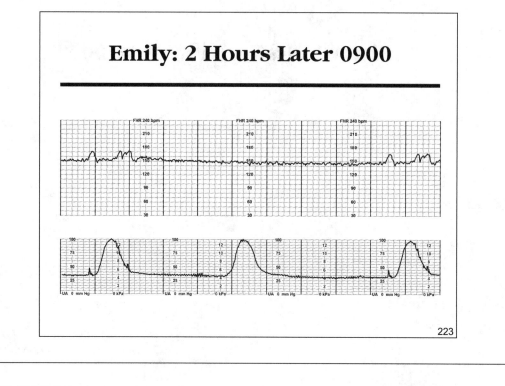

223

Emily: 2 Hours Later 0900

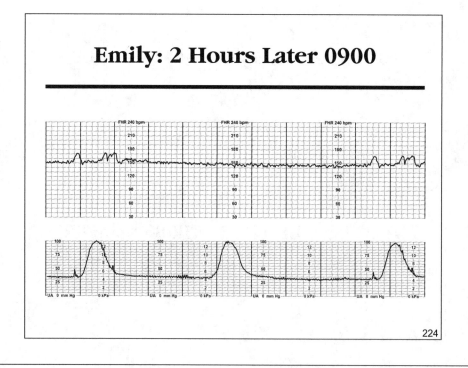

224

Emily: 2 Hours Later 1100

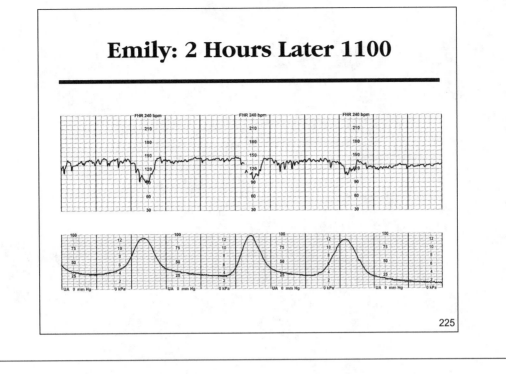

225

Emily: 1 Hour Later 1200

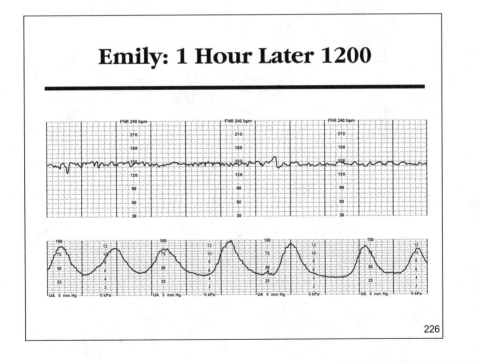

226

Emily: 1 Hour Later 1200

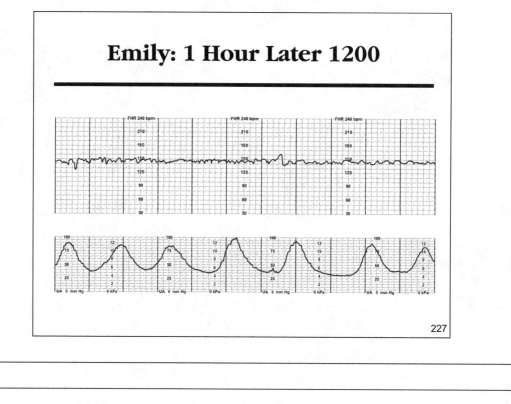

227

Emily: 30 Minutes Later 1230

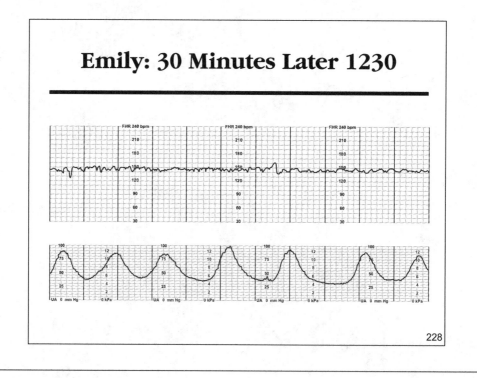

228

Emily: 2 Hours Later 1430

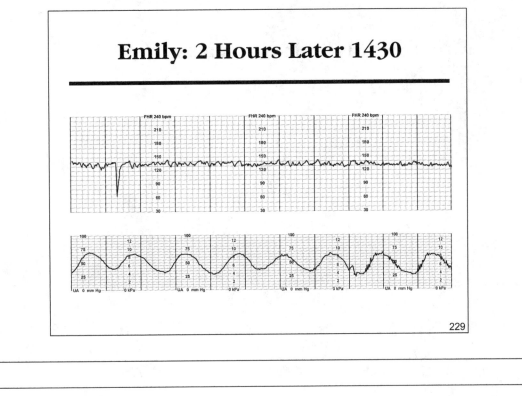

229

Emily: 2 Hours Later 1430

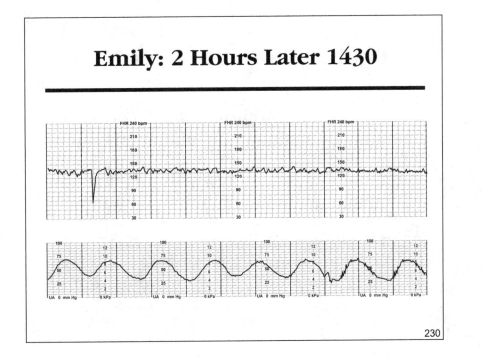

230

Emily: 2 Hours Later 1630

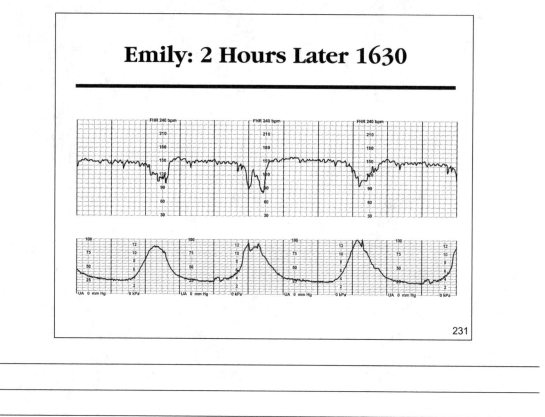

231

Emily: 45 Minutes Later 1715

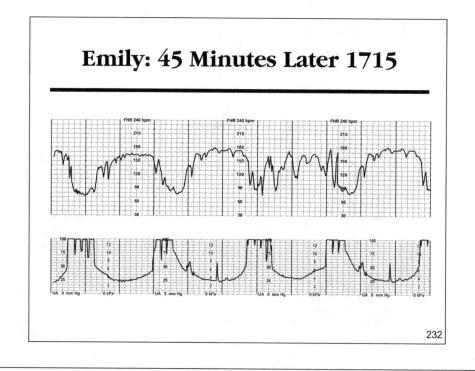

232

Emily: 45 Minutes Later 1715

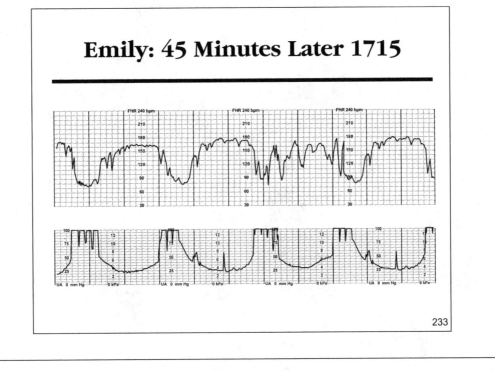

233

Emily: 10 Minutes Later 1725

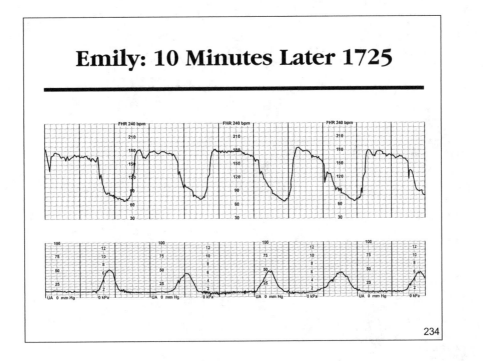

234

Emily

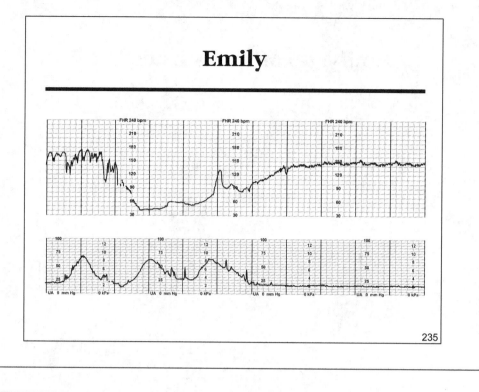

235

Emily: Outcome

Outcome
- Apgar scores 2 and 9

- Arterial cord gases
  - pH   7.01
  - pCO$_2$ 94
  - pO$_2$ 14
  - BE   −7.9

236

Maria Case Study

- 24 years old
- G_3P_{2002} at 36 4/7 weeks
- Two term vaginal births
- Regular prenatal care
- Normal prenatal labs
- No risk factors

237

Maria

- MVA, no apparent injuries
- Presents to OB triage
- VS: BP 120/64; HR 82 bpm; RR 16/min.; T 98.4° F

238

Maria: Initial Tracing

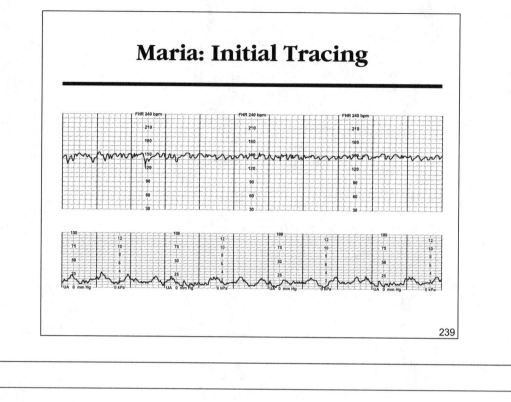

239

Maria: 1 Hour Later

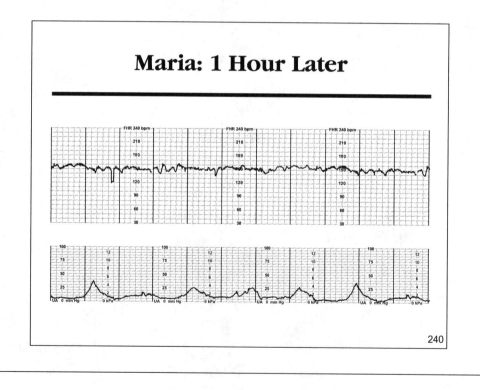

240

Maria: 3 Hours Later

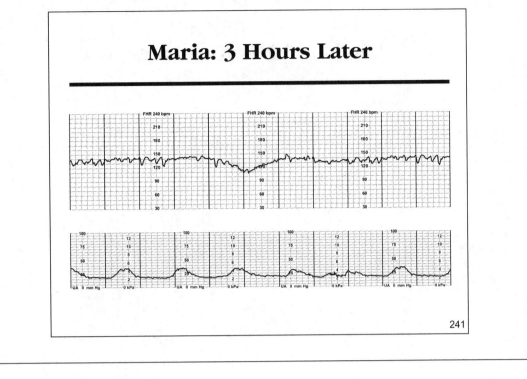

241

Maria: 30 Minutes Later

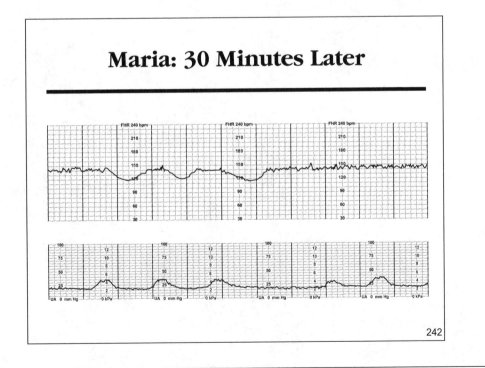

242

Maria: 30 Minutes Later

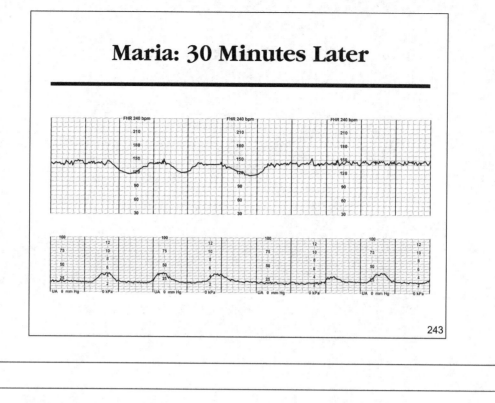

243

Maria: 45 Minutes Later

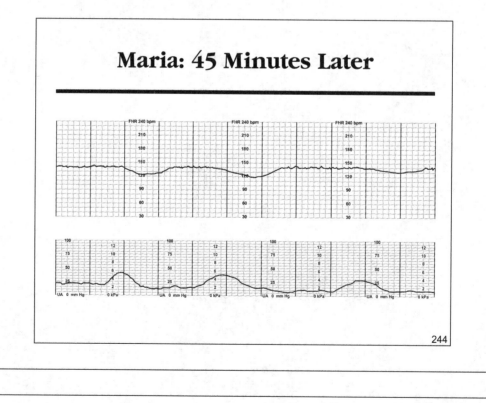

244

Maria: 45 Minutes Later

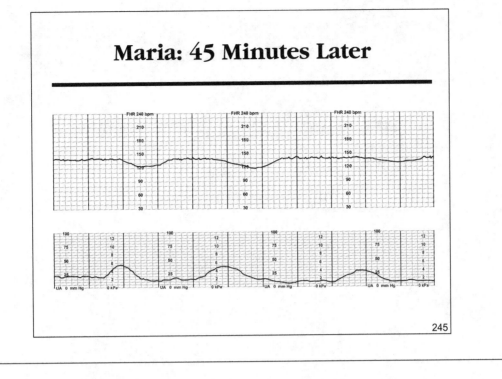

245

Maria: 20 Minutes Later

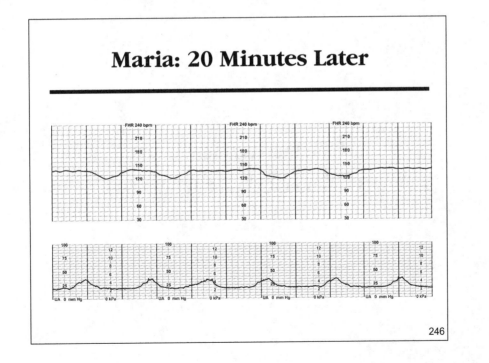

246

Maria: Outcome

- Stat Caesarean under general anesthesia

- Female infant

- Apgar scores of 2/6/7 at 1/5/10 minutes

- 40% placental abruption

247

Communication and Documentation

248

Communication

- Essential and central to quality care
- Influences patient safety, care, and outcomes for mothers and babies
- Channels should remain open in all directions
- Primary purpose: support high-quality care

249

Communication

- All of the providers on the perinatal team make important contributions
- The patient is at the center of communication and care
- Patient input should be encouraged and valued

250

Suggested Questions for Women

- What is most important to you today?
- Do you have a birth plan?
- What are your concerns about your care?
- Is there anything you are worried about that you'd like to discuss?
- Do you have any questions? Do you understand what is happening?

251

Communication

- Effective, patient-centered communication can contribute to reduction in medical-legal exposure

- Providing safe, quality care is one component of protection against legal liability

252

Communication With Professional Colleagues

- Each member of the health care team is valued for individual talents, education, experience, background, and perspective

- Trust, open communication, and effective interdisciplinary teamwork are integral to promoting safe patient care

253

Communication With Professional Colleagues

- Communication implies a transfer of information that ideally is accurate, timely, and conveyed with mutual respect

254

Barriers to Effective Communication

- Traditional roles of physicians and nurses
- Institutional territory and politics
- Different styles of learning
- Type and quantity of education
- Staffing levels
- Unresolved conflict

255

Strategies for Improving Communications Among Health Care Providers

- Effective communication is clear, direct, and explicit

- Effective communicators avoid indirect strategies

- Communication about FHR tracings should be conveyed using NICHD definitions

256

Structuring Communication

- S → Situation

- B → Background

- A → Assessment

- R → Recommendation

257

Structuring Communication

- S → Situation

- B → Background

- A → Assessment

- R → Recommendation

258

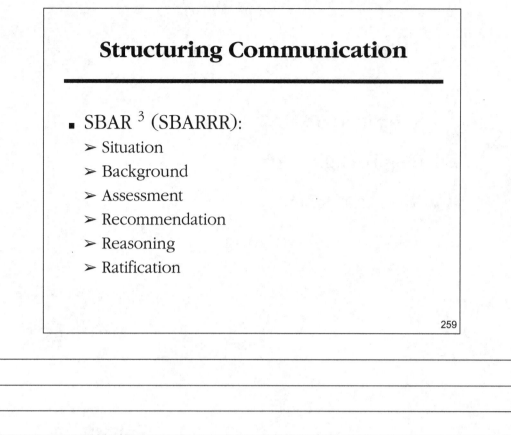

Structuring Communication

- SBAR [3] (SBARRR):
  - Situation
  - Background
  - Assessment
  - Recommendation
  - Reasoning
  - Ratification

259

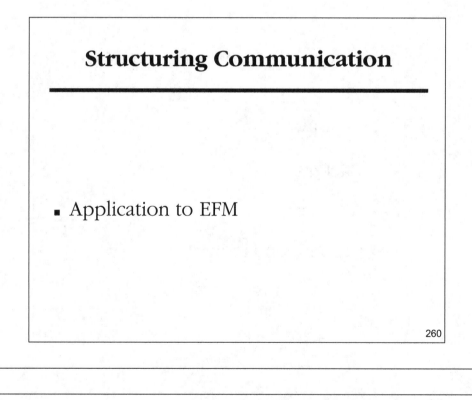

Structuring Communication

- Application to EFM

260

Structuring Communication

- Critical language:
  - ➤ Institution or unit-based word/phrase that signals the team to stop and assess the situation for safety
  - ➤ CUS:
    - Concerned
    - Uncomfortable
    - Safety

261

Hand-off Communication

- "Handoff" is the transfer of patient care from one care provider to another or from one type of unit, phase of care, or facility to another

- Standardized process of handoff communication has the potential to reduce communication breakdowns and to improve patient safety

262

Promoting Safe Hand-offs

- Use face to face communication if possible
- Develop protocols/tools that describe the information to be included in the handoff for each clinical situation
- Assess patient status together
- Limit interruptions
- During emergencies, remain involved until there is assurance that each piece of critical information has been accurately transferred and received

263

Hand-Off Tool

© M. Block, J. Ehrenworth, V, Cuce, N. Ng'ang'a, J. Weinback, S Saber, M. Schleisinger. "Tangible Handoff: a team approach for advancing structured communication in labor and delivery." Joint Commission Journal on Quality & Patient Safety. 36, 282–287, 241 (2010). Reprinted with permission.

264

Teamwork Practices that Enhance Communication

- Briefings
- Huddles
- Debriefings

265

Teamwork Practices that Enhance Communication

- Multidisciplinary rounds
- Multidisciplinary fetal heart monitoring education

266

Conflict and Conflict Management

- Occasional conflict is a fact of professional life
- Honest differences of opinion are expected
- It may not always be possible to resolve conflicts in a time-frame appropriate to the patient's condition
- Chain of command/authority/resolution is occasionally needed

267

Chain of Resolution

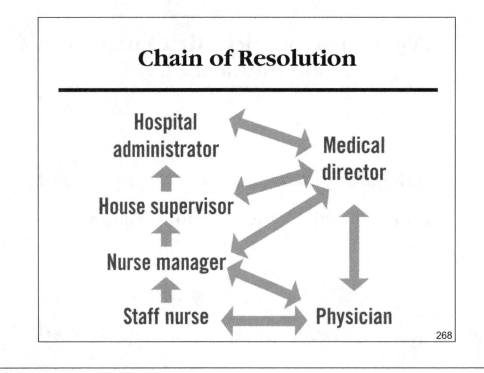

268

Effective Conflict Management

- Professionalism requires mutual respect and trust

- Disruptive behavior (rudeness, yelling, intimidation, etc.) does occur in some healthcare settings

269

Communication with Patients and Their Families or Support Persons

- Be respectful

- Involve the patient

- Support shared decision-making

270

Communication with Patients and Their Families or Support Persons

- Use translators and interpreters

271

Patient Teaching about FHM

- Inform woman and partner about purpose for and methods of fetal monitoring
- Discuss FHR tracing and usual baseline rate
- Discuss uterine contraction tracing and timing of contractions
- Explain volume control
- Explain positioning and implications for ambulation as appropriate
- Instruct how to notify the nurse

272

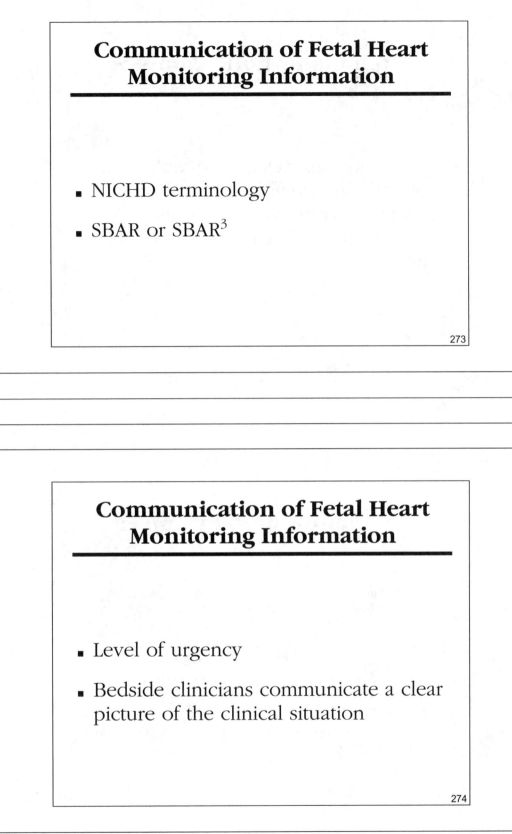

Communication of Fetal Heart Monitoring Information

- NICHD terminology
- SBAR or SBAR[3]

273

Communication of Fetal Heart Monitoring Information

- Level of urgency
- Bedside clinicians communicate a clear picture of the clinical situation

274

Communication Examples

"Hey, my patient's tracing looks kind of bad. The variability has gotten yucky and now there are some decelerations. Just wanted to let you know."

275

Communication Examples

"I am calling about Sarah Jones in room 4. She is completely dilated and +2 station with ruptured membranes. She is G4 P3003 at 39 weeks who presented in labor 30 minutes ago with a history of rapid labors. The FHR baseline is 145 bpm with moderate variability and recurrent variable decelerations that have not responded to position change. She has a strong urge to push. I need you to come now for imminent birth. When can I expect you at the bedside?"

276

Communicating Urgency

"I'm calling about Ms. Garcia, the patient we spoke about earlier. The FHR has a prolonged deceleration in the 90s for 3 minutes and has not resolved with interventions. I need you here now. When can I expect to see you?"

277

Documentation

- Main purpose is communication

- Achieving quality documentation:
  - Usability and efficiency of technology (EMR)
  - Unit documentation policies
  - Nurse-to-patient staffing ratios
  - Capabilities of the fetal monitoring system

278

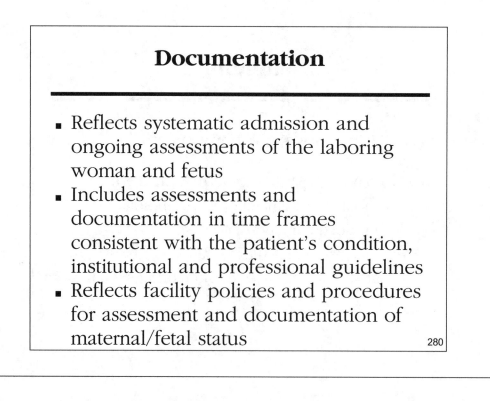

Documentation

- Streamlined, factual and objective record of the care provided
- Contains only and all clinically relevant information
- Duplication of information should be avoided:
  - ➤ Whenever possible, avoid documenting routine care on the EFM tracing when it is also being recorded in the chart
- Detailed description of tracings are unnecessary

279

Documentation

- Reflects systematic admission and ongoing assessments of the laboring woman and fetus
- Includes assessments and documentation in time frames consistent with the patient's condition, institutional and professional guidelines
- Reflects facility policies and procedures for assessment and documentation of maternal/fetal status

280

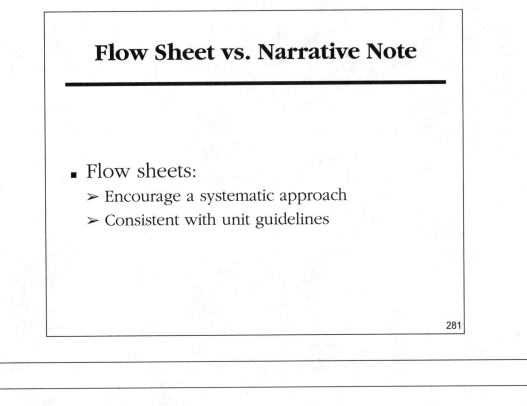

Flow Sheet vs. Narrative Note

- Flow sheets:
  - ➤ Encourage a systematic approach
  - ➤ Consistent with unit guidelines

281

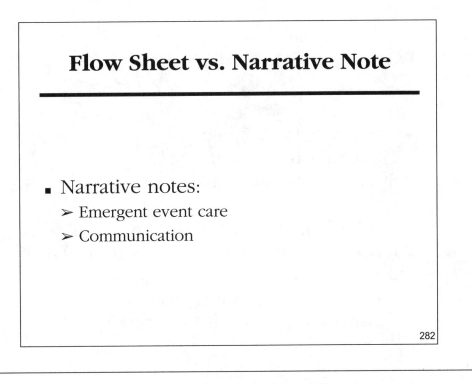

Flow Sheet vs. Narrative Note

- Narrative notes:
  - ➤ Emergent event care
  - ➤ Communication

282

Assessment of FHR

- Intermittent auscultation
- Electronic fetal monitoring

283

Documentation of Uterine Activity

- Frequency (in minutes)
- Duration (in seconds)
- Strength/intensity (mild, moderate, strong)
- Resting tone (level of firmness)
- Calculation of Montevideo Units (MVU)
  - ➤ Peak intensity minus resting tone of each contraction in 10-minute period
- Normal uterine activity vs. tachysystole

284

Identifying Information on Tracing

- Patient name

- Hospital identification number

- Date and time monitoring begun

- Mode of monitoring

- Calibration test, per facility protocol

285

Assessment vs. Documentation

Key points:
- Assessments are conducted at intervals appropriate to maternal–fetal condition

- Documentation may not have to occur at the same intervals as assessment

- Documentation should reflect a complete record of all assessments

286

EFM Tracing Analysis One

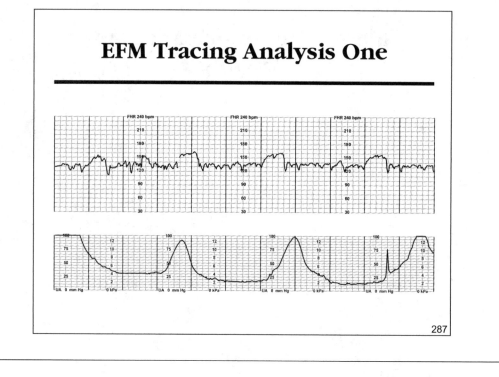

287

EFM Tracing Analysis Two

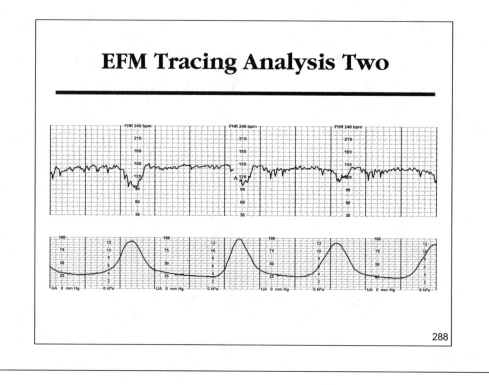

288

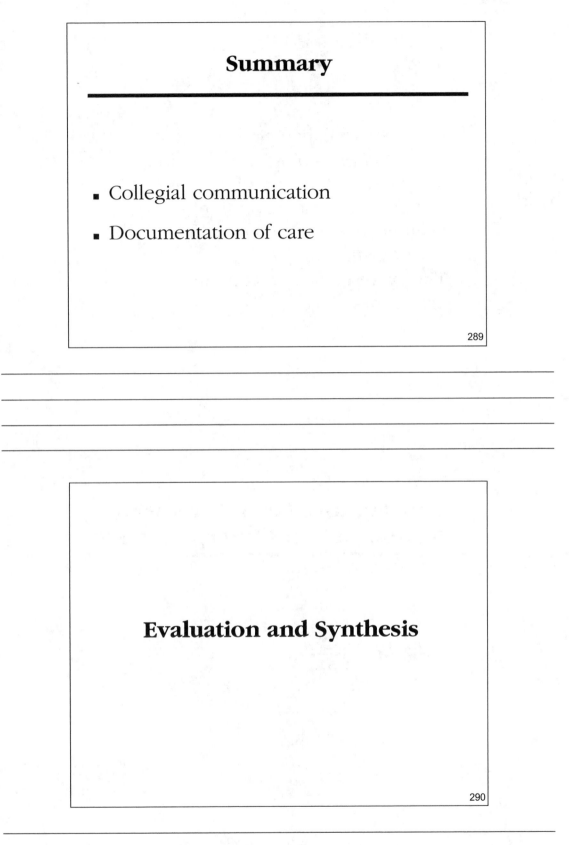

Summary

- Collegial communication
- Documentation of care

289

Evaluation and Synthesis

290

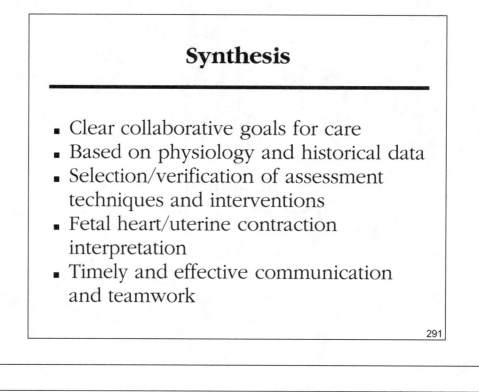

Synthesis

- Clear collaborative goals for care
- Based on physiology and historical data
- Selection/verification of assessment techniques and interventions
- Fetal heart/uterine contraction interpretation
- Timely and effective communication and teamwork

291

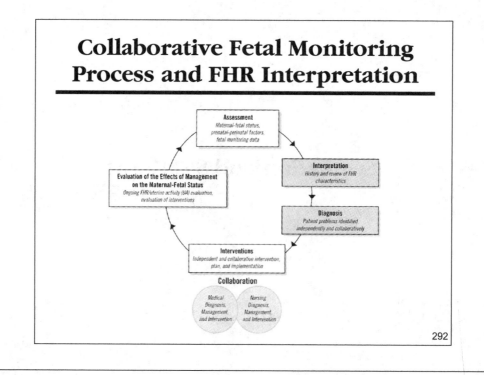

Collaborative Fetal Monitoring Process and FHR Interpretation

292

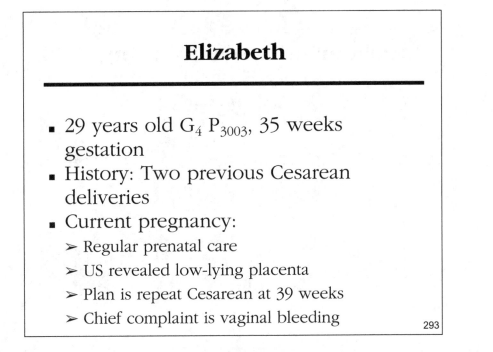

Elizabeth

- 29 years old G_4 P_{3003}, 35 weeks gestation
- History: Two previous Cesarean deliveries
- Current pregnancy:
  - ➤ Regular prenatal care
  - ➤ US revealed low-lying placenta
  - ➤ Plan is repeat Cesarean at 39 weeks
  - ➤ Chief complaint is vaginal bleeding

293

Elizabeth: Triage Assessment

- Assessed in triage for vaginal bleeding

- Vital signs: BP 124/68; P 80 bpm; R 18/min.; T 98.2°F (36.8°C)

- Abdomen palpates "soft"

- US and toco applied to assess FHR and uterine activity

294

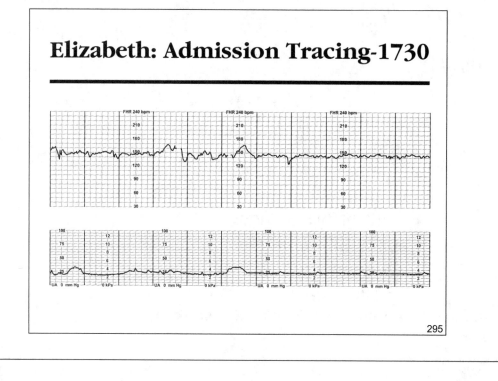

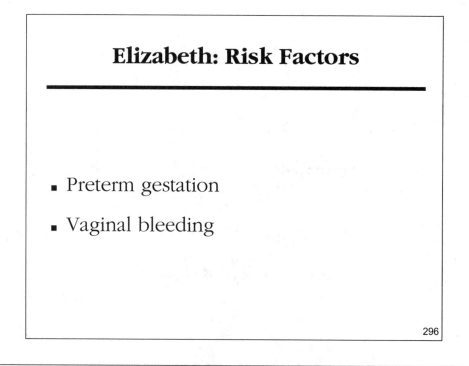

Elizabeth: 2000 (2½ Hours Later)

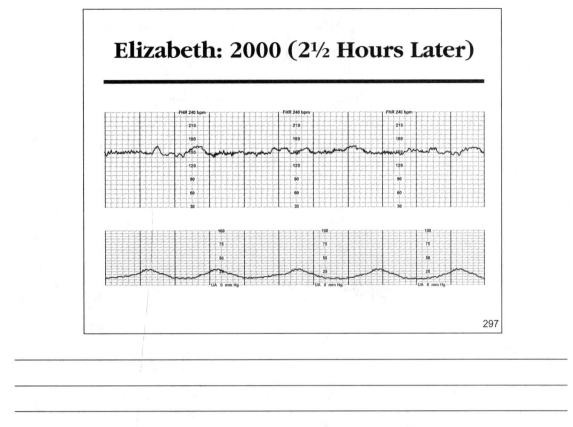

297

Elizabeth: 2300 (3 Hours Later)

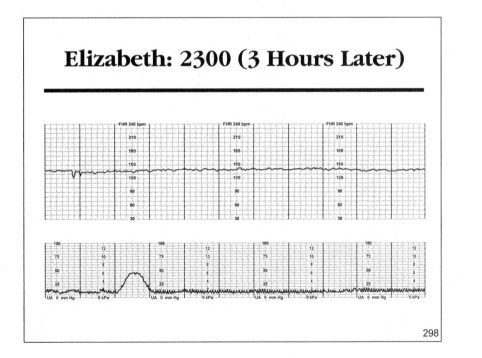

298

Elizabeth: 2300 (3 Hours Later)

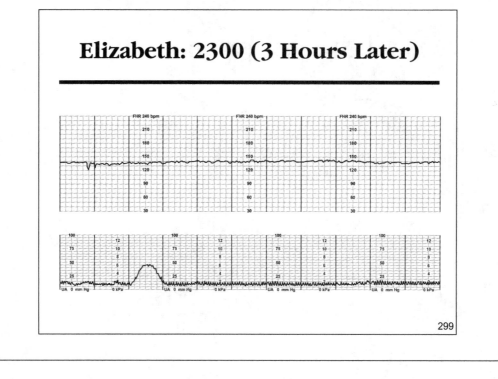

299

Elizabeth: 45 Minutes Later

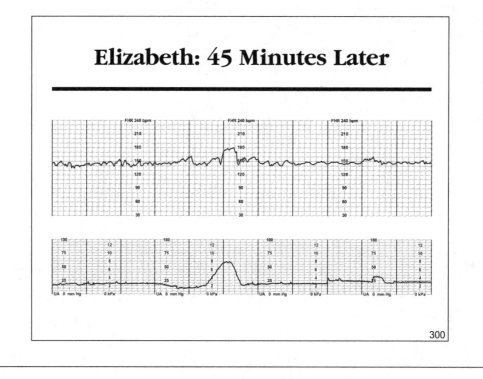

300

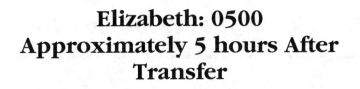

Elizabeth: 0500
Approximately 5 hours After Transfer

- Vaginal bleeding

- EFM initiated with US and toco

- Abdominal palpation

301

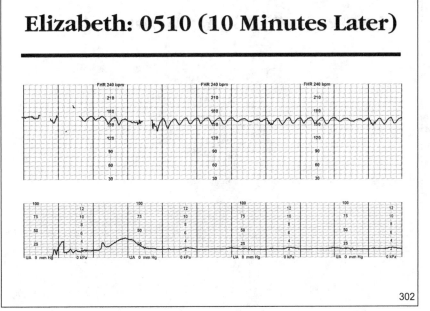

Elizabeth: 0510 (10 Minutes Later)

302

Elizabeth 0510 (10 Minutes Later)

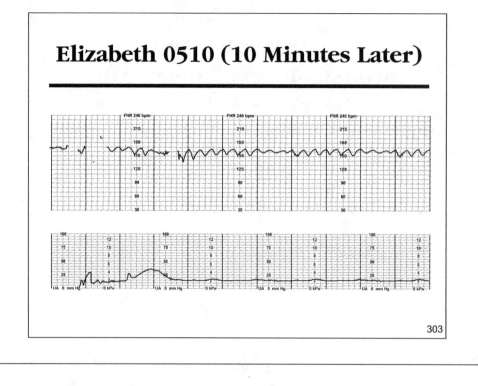

303

Elizabeth: 0520 (10 Minutes Later)

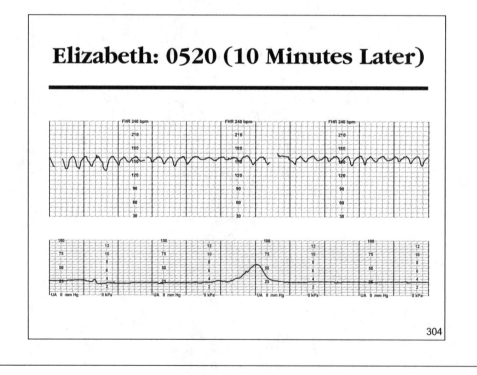

304

Elizabeth: 0520 (10 Minutes Later)

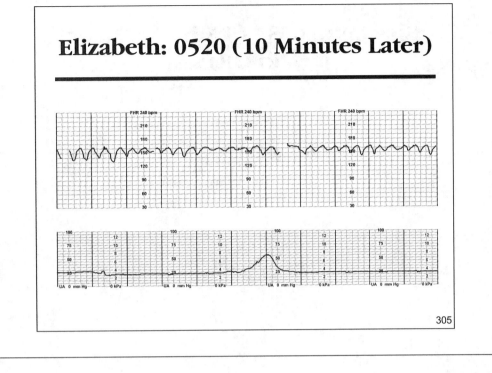

305

Elizabeth: 0530 (10 Minutes Later)

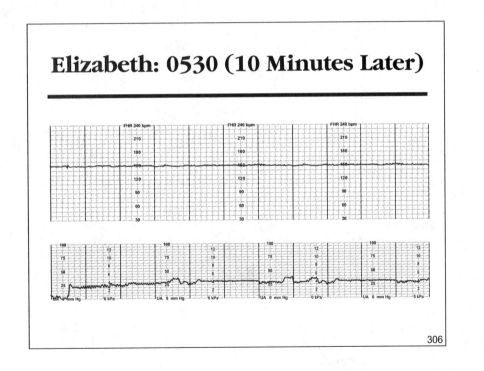

306

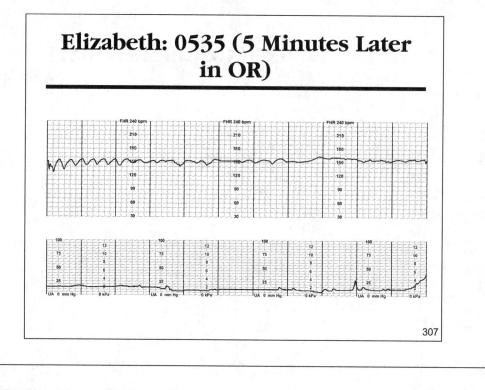

Elizabeth: 0535 (5 Minutes Later in OR)

307

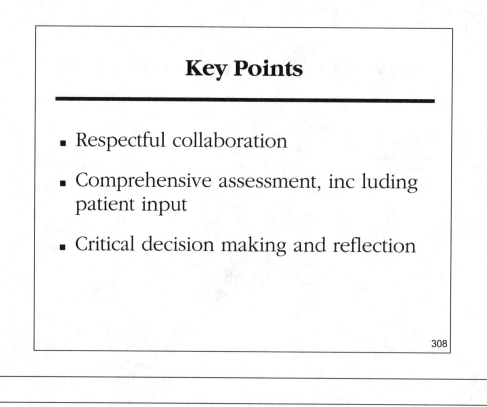

Key Points

- Respectful collaboration

- Comprehensive assessment, inc luding patient input

- Critical decision making and reflection

308

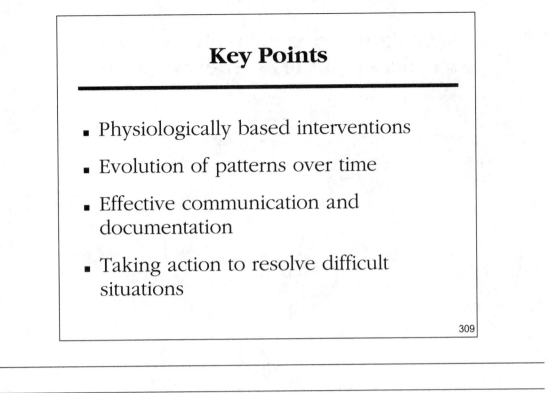

Key Points

- Physiologically based interventions
- Evolution of patterns over time
- Effective communication and documentation
- Taking action to resolve difficult situations

309

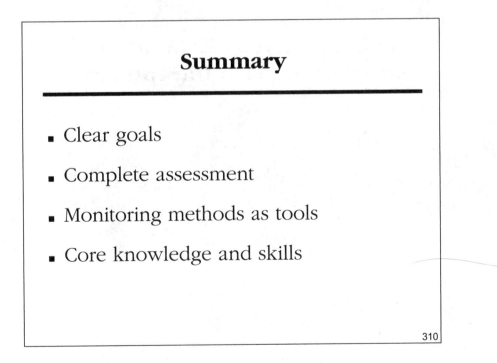

Summary

- Clear goals
- Complete assessment
- Monitoring methods as tools
- Core knowledge and skills

310

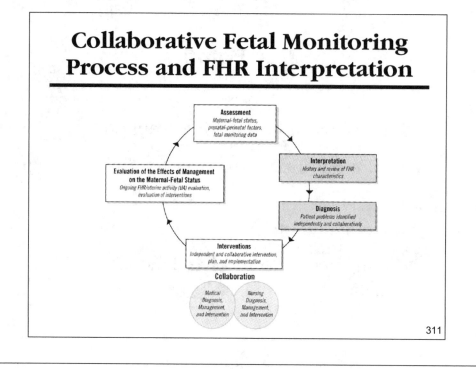

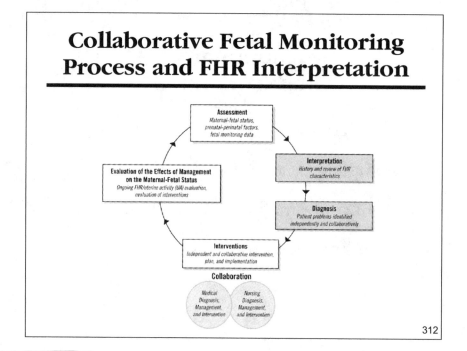

Disclaimer: This course and all accompanying materials (publication) were developed by AWHONN in cooperation with PESG, as an educational resource for fetal heart monitoring. It presents general methods and techniques of practice that are currently acceptable, based on current research and used by recognized authorities. Proper care of individual patients may depend on many individual factors to be considered in clinical practice, as well as professional judgment in the techniques described herein. Clinical circumstances naturally vary, and professionals must use their own best judgment in accordance with the patients' needs and preferences, professional standards and institutional rules. Variations and innovations that are consistent with law, and that demonstrably improve the quality of patient care, should be encouraged.

AWHONN has sought to confirm the accuracy of the information presented herein and to describe generally accepted practices. However, AWHONN is not responsible for errors or omissions or for any consequences from application of the information in this resource and makes no warranty, expressed or implied, with respect to the contents of the publication.

Competent clinical practice depends on a broad array of personal characteristics, training, judgment, professional skills, and institutional processes. This publication is simply one of many information resources. This publication is not intended to replace ongoing evaluation of knowledge and skills in the clinical setting. Nor has it been designed for use in hiring, promotion, or termination decisions or in resolving legal disputes or issues of liability.

AWHONN believes that drug selection and dosage set forth in this text are in accordance with current recommendations and practice at the time of publication. However, in view of ongoing research, changes in government regulations, and the constant flow of information relating to drug therapy and drug reactions, the reader is urged to check other information available in other published sources for each drug for potential changes in indications, dosages, and for added warnings, and precautions. This is particularly important when the recommended agent is a new or infrequently employed drug.

In addition, appropriate medication use may depend on unique factors such as individuals' health status, other medication use, and other factors which the professional must consider in clinical practice.

313

This portion of your book will be used during the skill stations exercises.

Please retain this book for your records and do not send it to AWHONN or to Professional Education Services Group.

Documentation Flowsheet

	TIME				
Cervix	Dilation				
	Effacement				
	Station				
Fetal Heart	Baseline Rate				
	Variability				
	Accelerations				
	Decelerations				
	STIM				
	Monitor Mode				
Uterine Activity	Frequency				
	Duration				
	Intensity				
	Resting Tone				
	Monitor Mode				
	Coping				
	Pain				
	Maternal Position				
	O_2/LPM/Mask				
	IV				
	Nurse Initials				

Date of Record: _____

AWHONN FETAL HEART MONITORING PROGRAM
SKILL STATION: INTEGRATION OF FETAL HEART MONITORING KNOWLEDGE AND PRACTICE
PRACTICE CASE ANSWER SHEET

CASE STUDY #_____

1. Baseline FHR: _____

2. Variability: a. absent (undetectable)   _____

                       b. minimal (>0 but <5 bpm)   _____

                       c. moderate (6–25 bpm)   _____

                       d. marked (>25 bpm)   _____

                       e. unable to determine   _____

3. Contractions: Frequency   _____

                       Duration   _____

                       Intensity   _____

                       Resting Tonus   _____

4. Accelerations and decelerations: When present, circle P if <u>periodic</u> and E if <u>episodic</u>.

Accelerations	P	E
Early decelerations	P	E
Variable decelerations	P	E
Late decelerations	P	E
Prolonged decelerations	P	E

5. List possible underlying physiologic mechanisms or rationales for observed patterns:

6. List actions and interventions indicated, based on overall interpretation (physiologic based, instrumentation based, and further assessments):

What category do the FHM characteristics fall into? _____

AWHONN FETAL HEART MONITORING PROGRAM

SKILL STATION: INTEGRATION OF FETAL HEART MONITORING KNOWLEDGE AND PRACTICE

PRACTICE CASE ANSWER SHEET

CASE STUDY #_____

1. Baseline FHR: _____

2. Variability:
   a. absent (undetectable) _____
   b. minimal (>0 but <5 bpm) _____
   c. moderate (6–25 bpm) _____
   d. marked (>25 bpm) _____
   e. unable to determine _____

3. Contractions:
   Frequency _____
   Duration _____
   Intensity _____
   Resting Tonus _____

4. Accelerations and decelerations: When present, circle P if <u>periodic</u> and E if <u>episodic</u>.

Accelerations	P	E
Early decelerations	P	E
Variable decelerations	P	E
Late decelerations	P	E
Prolonged decelerations	P	E

5. List possible underlying physiologic mechanisms or rationales for observed patterns:

6. List actions and interventions indicated, based on overall interpretation (physiologic based, instrumentation based, and further assessments):

   What category do the FHM characteristics fall into? _____

AWHONN FETAL HEART MONITORING PROGRAM

SKILL STATION: INTEGRATION OF FETAL HEART MONITORING KNOWLEDGE AND PRACTICE

PRACTICE CASE ANSWER SHEET

CASE STUDY #_____

1. Baseline FHR: _____

2. Variability: a. absent (undetectable)   _____

                   b. minimal (>0 but <5 bpm)   _____

                   c. moderate (6–25 bpm)   _____

                   d. marked (>25 bpm)   _____

                   e. unable to determine   _____

3. Contractions: Frequency   _____

                   Duration   _____

                   Intensity   _____

                   Resting Tonus   _____

4. Accelerations and decelerations: When present, circle P if <u>periodic</u> and E if <u>episodic</u>.

Accelerations	P	E
Early decelerations	P	E
Variable decelerations	P	E
Late decelerations	P	E
Prolonged decelerations	P	E

5. List possible underlying physiologic mechanisms or rationales for observed patterns:

6. List actions and interventions indicated, based on overall interpretation (physiologic based, instrumentation based, and further assessments):

   What category do the FHM characteristics fall into? _____

AWHONN FETAL HEART MONITORING PROGRAM

SKILL STATION: INTEGRATION OF FETAL HEART MONITORING KNOWLEDGE AND PRACTICE

PRACTICE CASE ANSWER SHEET

CASE STUDY #_____

1. Baseline FHR: _____

2. Variability: a. absent (undetectable)   _____

    b. minimal (>0 but <5 bpm)   _____

    c. moderate (6–25 bpm)   _____

    d. marked (>25 bpm)   _____

    e. unable to determine   _____

3. Contractions: Frequency   _____

    Duration   _____

    Intensity   _____

    Resting Tonus   _____

4. Accelerations and decelerations: When present, circle P if <u>periodic</u> and E if <u>episodic</u>.

Accelerations	P	E
Early decelerations	P	E
Variable decelerations	P	E
Late decelerations	P	E
Prolonged decelerations	P	E

5. List possible underlying physiologic mechanisms or rationales for observed patterns:

6. List actions and interventions indicated, based on overall interpretation (physiologic based, instrumentation based, and further assessments):

What category do the FHM characteristics fall into? _____

AWHONN FETAL HEART MONITORING PROGRAM

SKILL STATION: INTEGRATION OF FETAL HEART MONITORING KNOWLEDGE AND PRACTICE

PRACTICE CASE ANSWER SHEET

CASE STUDY #_____

1. Baseline FHR: _____

2. Variability:
   - a. absent (undetectable) _____
   - b. minimal (>0 but <5 bpm) _____
   - c. moderate (6–25 bpm) _____
   - d. marked (>25 bpm) _____
   - e. unable to determine _____

3. Contractions:
   - Frequency _____
   - Duration _____
   - Intensity _____
   - Resting Tonus _____

4. Accelerations and decelerations: When present, circle P if <u>periodic</u> and E if <u>episodic</u>.

Accelerations	P	E
Early decelerations	P	E
Variable decelerations	P	E
Late decelerations	P	E
Prolonged decelerations	P	E

5. List possible underlying physiologic mechanisms or rationales for observed patterns:

6. List actions and interventions indicated, based on overall interpretation (physiologic based, instrumentation based, and further assessments):

   What category do the FHM characteristics fall into? _____

AWHONN FETAL HEART MONITORING PROGRAM

SKILL STATION: INTEGRATION OF FETAL HEART MONITORING KNOWLEDGE AND PRACTICE

PRACTICE CASE ANSWER SHEET

CASE STUDY #_____

1. Baseline FHR: _____

2. Variability:
   a. absent (undetectable) _____
   b. minimal (>0 but <5 bpm) _____
   c. moderate (6–25 bpm) _____
   d. marked (>25 bpm) _____
   e. unable to determine _____

3. Contractions:
   Frequency _____
   Duration _____
   Intensity _____
   Resting Tonus _____

4. Accelerations and decelerations: When present, circle P if _periodic_ and E if _episodic_.

Accelerations	P	E
Early decelerations	P	E
Variable decelerations	P	E
Late decelerations	P	E
Prolonged decelerations	P	E

5. List possible underlying physiologic mechanisms or rationales for observed patterns:

6. List actions and interventions indicated, based on overall interpretation (physiologic based, instrumentation based, and further assessments):

What category do the FHM characteristics fall into? _____

AWHONN FETAL HEART MONITORING PROGRAM
SKILL STATION: INTEGRATION OF FETAL HEART MONITORING KNOWLEDGE AND PRACTICE
PRACTICE CASE ANSWER SHEET

CASE STUDY #_____

1. Baseline FHR: _____

2. Variability:
   a. absent (undetectable) _____
   b. minimal (>0 but <5 bpm) _____
   c. moderate (6–25 bpm) _____
   d. marked (>25 bpm) _____
   e. unable to determine _____

3. Contractions:
   Frequency _____
   Duration _____
   Intensity _____
   Resting Tonus _____

4. Accelerations and decelerations: When present, circle P if <u>periodic</u> and E if <u>episodic</u>.

Accelerations	P	E
Early decelerations	P	E
Variable decelerations	P	E
Late decelerations	P	E
Prolonged decelerations	P	E

5. List possible underlying physiologic mechanisms or rationales for observed patterns:

6. List actions and interventions indicated, based on overall interpretation (physiologic based, instrumentation based, and further assessments):

   What category do the FHM characteristics fall into? _____

AWHONN FETAL HEART MONITORING PROGRAM

SKILL STATION: INTEGRATION OF FETAL HEART MONITORING
KNOWLEDGE AND PRACTICE

PRACTICE CASE ANSWER SHEET

CASE STUDY #____

1. Baseline FHR: ____

2. Variability: a. absent (undetectable)   ____

                       b. minimal (>0 but <5 bpm)   ____

                       c. moderate (6–25 bpm)   ____

                       d. marked (>25 bpm)   ____

                       e. unable to determine   ____

3. Contractions: Frequency   ____

                    Duration   ____

                    Intensity   ____

                    Resting Tonus   ____

4. Accelerations and decelerations: When present, circle P if <u>periodic</u> and E if <u>episodic</u>.

Accelerations	P	E
Early decelerations	P	E
Variable decelerations	P	E
Late decelerations	P	E
Prolonged decelerations	P	E

5. List possible underlying physiologic mechanisms or rationales for observed patterns:

6. List actions and interventions indicated, based on overall interpretation (physiologic based, instrumentation based, and further assessments):

   What category do the FHM characteristics fall into? _____

AWHONN FETAL HEART MONITORING PROGRAM

SKILL STATION: INTEGRATION OF FETAL HEART MONITORING KNOWLEDGE AND PRACTICE

PRACTICE CASE ANSWER SHEET

CASE STUDY #____

1. Baseline FHR: ____

2. Variability: a. absent (undetectable)   ____

                     b. minimal (>0 but <5 bpm)   ____

                     c. moderate (6–25 bpm)   ____

                     d. marked (>25 bpm)   ____

                     e. unable to determine   ____

3. Contractions: Frequency   ____

                    Duration   ____

                    Intensity   ____

                    Resting Tonus   ____

4. Accelerations and decelerations: When present, circle P if <u>periodic</u> and E if <u>episodic</u>.

Accelerations	P	E
Early decelerations	P	E
Variable decelerations	P	E
Late decelerations	P	E
Prolonged decelerations	P	E

5. List possible underlying physiologic mechanisms or rationales for observed patterns:

6. List actions and interventions indicated, based on overall interpretation (physiologic based, instrumentation based, and further assessments):

   What category do the FHM characteristics fall into? _____

AWHONN FETAL HEART MONITORING PROGRAM

SKILL STATION: INTEGRATION OF FETAL HEART MONITORING KNOWLEDGE AND PRACTICE

PRACTICE CASE ANSWER SHEET

CASE STUDY #____

1. Baseline FHR: ____

2. Variability: a. absent (undetectable) ____

                  b. minimal (>0 but <5 bpm) ____

                  c. moderate (6–25 bpm) ____

                  d. marked (>25 bpm) ____

                  e. unable to determine ____

3. Contractions: Frequency ____

                  Duration ____

                  Intensity ____

                  Resting Tonus ____

4. Accelerations and decelerations: When present, circle P if <u>periodic</u> and E if <u>episodic</u>.

Accelerations	P	E
Early decelerations	P	E
Variable decelerations	P	E
Late decelerations	P	E
Prolonged decelerations	P	E

5. List possible underlying physiologic mechanisms or rationales for observed patterns:

6. List actions and interventions indicated, based on overall interpretation (physiologic based, instrumentation based, and further assessments):

What category do the FHM characteristics fall into? _____

AWHONN FETAL HEART MONITORING PROGRAM
SKILL STATION: INTEGRATION OF FETAL HEART MONITORING
KNOWLEDGE AND PRACTICE
PRACTICE CASE ANSWER SHEET

CASE STUDY #_____

1. Baseline FHR: _____

2. Variability: a. absent (undetectable)   _____

                b. minimal (>0 but <5 bpm)   _____

                c. moderate (6–25 bpm)   _____

                d. marked (>25 bpm)   _____

                e. unable to determine   _____

3. Contractions: Frequency   _____

                Duration   _____

                Intensity   _____

                Resting Tonus   _____

4. Accelerations and decelerations: When present, circle P if periodic and E if episodic.

Accelerations	P	E
Early decelerations	P	E
Variable decelerations	P	E
Late decelerations	P	E
Prolonged decelerations	P	E

5. List possible underlying physiologic mechanisms or rationales for observed patterns:

6. List actions and interventions indicated, based on overall interpretation (physiologic based, instrumentation based, and further assessments):

What category do the FHM characteristics fall into? _____

SKILL STATION: COMMUNICATION OF FETAL HEART MONITORING DATA PRACTICE

Practice Exercise I

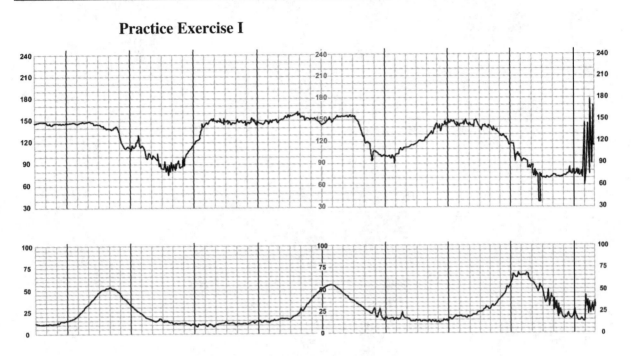

The data on this tracing segment was obtained using ultrasound and toco.

Baseline rate   150

Variability   mod min

Accelerations   —

Decelerations   Variables + lates

Uterine activity   3 min 70-80 sec

Discuss what you would report to your clinician colleagues.

What category do these characteristics fall into?   Category II

Communication Practice Exercise I
Responses

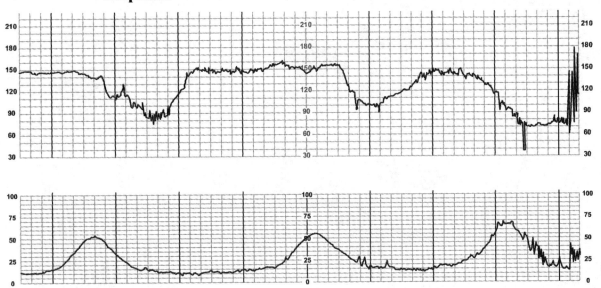

Baseline rate   150 bpm

Variability   minimal

Accelerations   none

Decelerations   late and variable

Discuss what you would report to your clinician colleagues.

The FHR baseline is 150 bpm with minimal variability and recurrent late and periodic variable decelerations. The tracing requires your immediate bedside evaluation. When can I expect you to be here?

Category II characteristics

Communication Practice Exercise II

Please document the interpretation of this tracing segment using the flow sheet in your Student Materials book.

This data has been obtained via fetal spiral electrode and intrauterine pressure catheter.

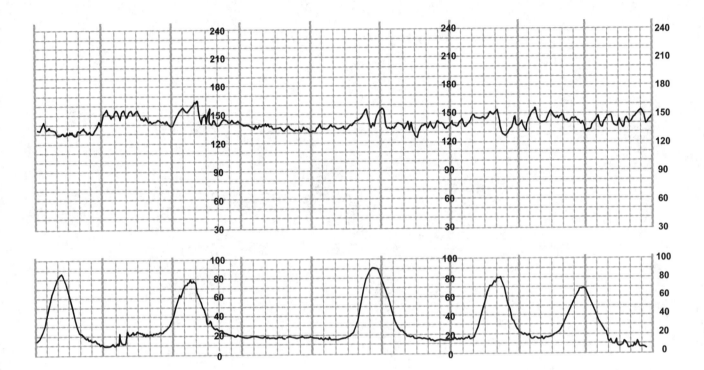

Practice Exercise II—Documentation Flow sheet

Date of Record: _____

		TIME			
Cervix	Dilation				
	Effacement				
	Station				
Fetal Heart	Baseline Rate				
	Variability				
	Accelerations				
	Decelerations				
	STIM				
	Monitor Mode				
Uterine Activity	Frequency				
	Duration				
	Intensity				
	Resting Tone				
	Monitor Mode				
	Coping				
	Maternal Position				
	O_2/LPM/Mask				
	IV				
Nurse Initials					

Practice Exercise II—Documentation

Date of Record: _____

	TIME				
Cervix	Dilation				
	Effacement				
	Station				
Fetal Heart	Variability	Moderate			
	Baseline Rate	140			
	Accelerations	Present			
	Decelerations	Ø			
	STIM				
	Monitor Mode	FSE			
Uterine Activity	Frequency	1–3			
	Duration	40–50			
	Intensity	70–90			
	Resting Tone	10–15			
	Monitor Mode	IUPC			
	Coping				
	Maternal Position				
	O$_2$/LPM/Mask				
	IV				
	Nurse Initials				

SKILL STATION: COMMUNICATION OF FETAL HEART MONITORING DATA TEST—MONICA

NOTE: There are two separate exercises in the testing component of this station (Part I relates to Monica and Part II relates to the Communication video). Please do both of them.

Part I-Monica (See the tracings and flow sheet on the following pages)

Monica is a G3T2P0A0L2 admitted in early labor at 39 weeks gestation. No risk factors are noted, no antepartum testing was done. She had two previous low risk pregnancies; these children are ages 8 and 10 years old. Her vaginal exam reveals a 3 cm, 90% effaced, floating, and cephalic presentation. Membranes are intact. U/S and toco monitors are in place.

Instructions

A. Interpret the monitor tracings on the next page and document your findings in two separate columns on the flow sheet provided. Please include any additional trouble-shooting or interventions you would provide in the appropriate spaces in the flow sheet.

B. Assume that after the second monitor tracing at 1530 you provide telephone report to Monica's physician to describe the observed pattern. You are told to call again in 1 hour if there is no change. Document your short verbal response to the physician in the space below and also describe the next clinical action you will take in response to the physician's order. Take the scenario as far as you believe is appropriate.

Part I—Monica
U/S, TOCO

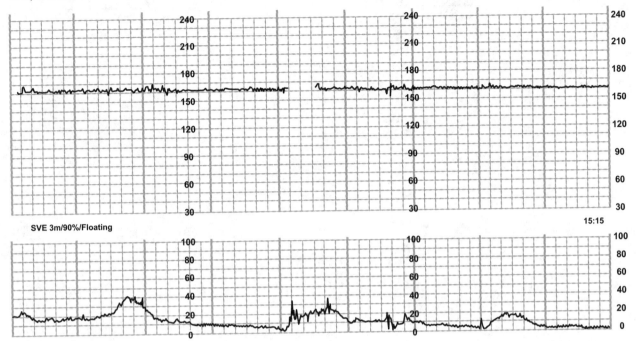

SVE 3m/90%/Floating

15:15

Part II, (Monica, cont.)
FSE, TOCO

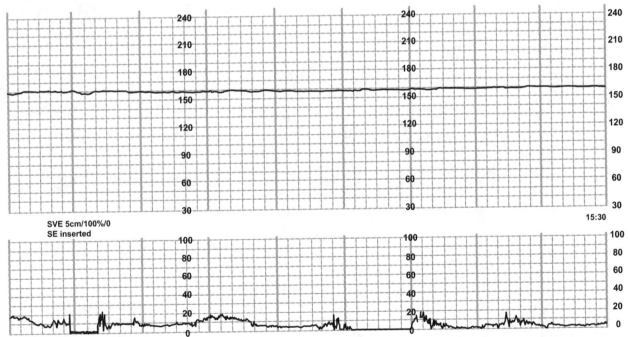

SVE 5cm/100%/0
SE inserted

15:30

Part I—Monica Case Study and EFM Tracing

Documentation Flow sheet

Date of Record: _____

		TIME			
Cervix	Dilation				
	Effacement				
	Station				
Fetal Heart	Baseline Rate				
	Variability				
	Accelerations				
	Decelerations				
	STIM				
	Monitor Mode				
	Frequency				
Uterine Activity	Duration				
	Intensity				
	Resting Tone				
	Monitor Mode				
	Coping				
	Pain				
	Maternal Position				
	O_2/LPM/Mask				
	IV				
Nurse Initials					

Documentation Flow sheet

		TIME	1315	1530		
Cervix	Dilation		3	5		
Cervix	Effacement		90	100		
Cervix	Station		float	0		
Fetal Heart	Baseline Rate		160	160		
Fetal Heart	Variability		min	ab		
Fetal Heart	Accelerations		—	—		
Fetal Heart	Decelerations		—			
Fetal Heart	STIM					
Fetal Heart	Monitor Mode					
Uterine Activity	Frequency		3min			
Uterine Activity	Duration		40-50			
Uterine Activity	Intensity					
Uterine Activity	Resting Tone					
Uterine Activity	Monitor Mode					
	Coping					
	Pain					
	Maternal Position					
	O$_2$/LPM/Mask					
	IV					
Nurse Initials						

Documentation Flowsheet

Date of Record: _____

		TIME				
Cervix	Dilation					
	Effacement					
	Station					
Fetal Heart	Baseline Rate					
	Variability					
	Accelerations					
	Decelerations					
	STIM					
	Monitor Mode					
Uterine Activity	Frequency					
	Duration					
	Intensity					
	Resting Tone					
	Monitor Mode					
	Coping					
	Pain					
	Maternal Position					
	O_2/LPM/Mask					
	IV					
Nurse Initials						

NOTE: This is the second part of the communication skill station.

Part II—Communication Video

For this exercise you will watch several scenarios depicting communications among clinicians. The scenarios can be viewed more than once if needed. The objective of the testing component of the DVD is that you will document four omissions you noted in the segment assigned by the course Instructor. There are more than four omissions in the scenario, but you are only required to list four.

1. _____

2. _____

3. _____

4. _____

SKILL STATION: COMMUNICATION SCENARIO CRITIQUE WORKSHEET

Please use this page to list your answers for the critique of communication about fetal heart monitoring information (you may write on the back of the page if needed).

Nurse-to-Nurse Report
Data included in the report:

_____

_____

_____

_____

_____

_____

_____

Nurse-to-Nurse Report
Data omitted from the report:

_____

_____

_____

_____

_____

_____

_____

Nurse-to-Patient Education
Data included in the education:

_____

_____

_____

_____

_____

Nurse-to-Patient Education
Data that may have been added:

_____

_____

_____

_____

_____

Nurse-to-Physician Report
Data included in the report:

_____

_____

_____

_____

_____

_____

_____

Nurse-to-Physician Report
Data omitted from the report:

_____

_____

_____

_____

_____

_____

_____

Nurse-to-Patient Education
Data included in the education:

_____

_____

_____

_____

_____

Nurse-to-Physician Report
Data included in the report:

_____

_____

_____

_____

_____

_____

_____

_____

_____

Nurse-to-Charge Nurse Report
Data included in the report:

_____

_____

_____

_____

_____

_____

_____

Nurse-to-Patient Education
Data that may have been added:

_____

_____

_____

_____

_____

Nurse-to-Physician Report
Data omitted from the report:

_____

_____

_____

_____

_____

_____

_____

_____

_____

Nurse-to-Charge Nurse Report
Data omitted from the report:

_____

_____

_____

_____

_____

_____

_____

Charge Nurse-to-Nurse Manager Report

Data included in the report:

_____

_____

_____

_____

_____

_____

_____

Charge Nurse-to-Manager Report

Data omitted from the report:

_____

_____

_____

_____

_____

_____

_____